POCKET BOOK OF

BIRDS

PETER HOLDEN

PHOTOGRAPHIC CONSULTANT

PAUL STERRY

HarperCollins*Publishers*

This edition published
in 2002 exclusively for
WHSmith, Greenbridge
Road, Swindon SN3 3LD

First published 1996

Title page photograph: Kingfisher, *Alcedo atthis*

Artwork by Norman Arlott

ISBN 000 7660154

Edited and designed by D & N Publishing
Printed and bound by Printing Express Ltd., Hong Kong

WHY WATCH BIRDS?

I have watched birds for more than forty years, but I still find it difficult to explain their fascination. Their immense variety, extreme beauty and amazing behaviour are just some of the reasons. Their ability to span the world on their migrations and to adapt to live in all environments including hot dry deserts, the open oceans or even the ice cap of Antarctica, captures and fires my imagination.

Fortunately it is not necessary to travel to remote areas to see some of these remarkable birds. The first Swallow of spring is the survivor of a great journey which has taken it from the British Isles to South Africa and back. The Knots which flock to our estuaries in autumn are migrants from beyond the Arctic Circle, and the solitary Wheatear on a sea-cliff in spring may be en route from its winter quarters south of the Sahara to its Greenland nesting site.

Even our garden birds are a source of inspiration: the Song Thrush cracking open snails on the garden path, the Robin's fierce defence of its territory, the House Martins which build their mud nests under the eaves, and the dramatic Sparrowhawk which has almost recovered from the effects of agricultural chemicals and now hunts small birds – even in our gardens – with breath-taking agility.

In our modern world, we can become increasingly isolated from nature, but birds are an ever-present link with the natural world and, rather like the miners' canary, can indicate just how healthy our planet is.

It was the dramatic decline in birds of prey after World War II that first alerted the public to the dangers of pesticides in the environment, and more recently the fluctuations in populations of farmland birds have demonstrated the effect of modern farming methods.

But the best reason for watching birds is simply pleasure. It's fun! Birds are everywhere and we can enjoy them wherever we live. It is a hobby that has no end; it can involve both the young and the 'not so young' and it can last a lifetime.

HOW TO USE THIS BOOK

This book is a basic introduction to the birds you are likely to encounter in the British Isles and most of them will also be found in the other countries bordering the North Sea. It is intended to be taken out into the field, either in a pocket or on the dashboard of a car. Its first purpose is to help you identify the birds you see and secondly to tell you a little more about them.

Over 240 species are described, and these were chosen because they occur either as breeding species or as migrants which arrive here for the winter. There are a few others which are neither breeding nor wintering species: these are the 'passage migrants' which visit the British Isles during their migrations.

It was difficult to decide which passage migrants to include, as a great many birds will occasionally visit these islands either en route to somewhere else or having been blown off course. On the whole I chose those which occur either in reasonable numbers in some years or those which are seen in smaller numbers almost every year.

The **photographs** show the birds in the plumage you are most likely to see them in and behaving in a typical way. For example, many of the birds of prey are shown in flight because that is how they are nearly always seen by people walking in the countryside.

In addition to the photographs there are **illustrations** which show other common plumages, such as the female, a young bird or the winter plumage. So if the photograph does not quite match what you are seeing, remember to check the illustrations as well.

The information is set out in a similar way for each bird. The sections are as follows:

Measurements: always in centimetres to allow comparisons. These are measurements as used by scientists and are taken from dead specimens laid on their back and measured from tip of bill to tip of tail.

Name: the usual name in English.

Scientific name: derived from Latin or Greek and used the world over.

Main text: introduction to the bird, its habitat, its food, its range in Europe and nesting information.

ID FACT FILE – gives information at a glance.

Size: compared with common species.

Description: giving all the common plumages of both adults and young.

Bill: a description of the birds bill, or beak, which is often a good clue to its feeding habits and helpful for identification.

Flight: what features to look for in flight.

Voice: really difficult to describe, but an attempt to help the reader to recognise both songs and common calls.

Lookalikes: any other species with which the species could be confused.

Also at the top of each page is a silhouette of a bird. This is a code to help you recognise which family or group the bird is in. These are as follows:

Divers and grebes (pp.9–16)

Shearwaters and petrels (pp.17–23)

Gannet and cormorants (pp.24–26)

Herons and allies (pp.27–30)

Swans, geese and ducks (pp.31–63)

Birds of prey (pp.64–79)

Game birds and rails (pp.80–91)

Waders (pp.92–122)

Skuas, gulls and terns (pp.123–39)

Auks (pp.140–4)

Pigeons (pp.145–9)

Cuckoo (p.150), Nightjar (p.157)

Ring-necked Parakeet (p.151)

Owls (pp.152–6)

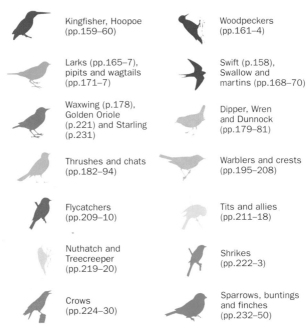

Kingfisher, Hoopoe (pp.159–60)

Woodpeckers (pp.161–4)

Larks (pp.165–7), pipits and wagtails (pp.171–7)

Swift (p.158), Swallow and martins (pp.168–70)

Waxwing (p.178), Golden Oriole (p.221) and Starling (p.231)

Dipper, Wren and Dunnock (pp.179–81)

Thrushes and chats (pp.182–94)

Warblers and crests (pp.195–208)

Flycatchers (pp.209–10)

Tits and allies (pp.211–18)

Nuthatch and Treecreeper (pp.219–20)

Shrikes (pp.222–3)

Crows (pp.224–30)

Sparrows, buntings and finches (pp.232–50)

The maps. The fact that birds are highly mobile is one of the fascinations of birdwatching. Usually, however, they are restricted by habitat and food and it is therefore possible to map where they are most likely to be found. On the maps, the red areas represent the bird's breeding range. The area below the heavy dotted line, or enclosed by it, is the bird's winter range. This does not mean that the bird occurs everywhere within these limits, but locally where its proper habitat is available. If the bird's winter range is identical to its breeding range, or if the bird leaves the area entirely in winter there is no dotted line. Remember that birds are usually more likely to travel outside the breeding season and when on migration.

The **time bar** gives a month-by-month guide to when you can expect to see the birds. Dark green indicates the months in which the bird definitely occurs in Britain; mid-green means it may occur; light green is used when it does not occur.

HOW TO WATCH BIRDS

The great advantage of birdwatching over other hobbies is that you need very little equipment. It is possible to get close to birds in gardens and parks without needing any equipment at all.
Binoculars: the first and most important purchase is a pair of binoculars. These need not be too expensive, but it is good advice not to choose the very cheapest. The secret is to try several pairs out, preferably out of doors, until you find a pair which suits your eyes and pocket!

There are a few tips, however. The most powerful binoculars are not necessarily the best, because they have a small field of view and magnify hand-shake and wind-shake. Binocular specifications such as 7×42, 8×30 and 10×40 are the type most commonly used by birdwatchers. (The first number is the magnification, the second the diameter of the larger lens in millimetres.) Remember that if they are going to hang round your neck on a long walk, then their weight is also an important factor.
Telescopes: these help the birdwatcher to get even better views, but they need a sturdy tripod to keep them rigid and together this makes a great deal of extra equipment to carry. Telescopes are best left until the observer is more experienced and familiar with many of the more common species.

WHERE TO GO

Local habitats: part of the fun of watching birds and, indeed, the start of more serious ornithology, is getting to know your local birds. Perhaps your local spot will be a park, a lake, an area of farmland; somewhere you can watch the changes throughout the seasons. Keep notes of the different species, when migrants arrive and depart, which birds breed and which only visit; this is the start of a proper survey and can help conservationists if ever the area is threatened with change.
Nature reserves are places which are specially managed for birds and other wildlife. Many of them are open to the public and are good places to see both common and less common species. Often there are staff or volunteers to help visitors

identify the birds and explain why the area is so valuable. Many reserves need the help of volunteers to carry out simple tasks which are essential for the wildlife. This can be a splendid introduction for the beginner and also for the more experienced. Working alongside more knowledgeable people is the best way to learn.

Join a group or club: there are many local and national organisations that arrange excursions and indoor meetings. Taking part is another good way to learn more. In some localities there are evening or daytime classes in ornithology and the benefit of an expert can be an invaluable help to the new recruit.

CONSERVATION

The hobby takes on a new dimension when we start to consider the changes to our countryside. Many birds are disappearing from places where they were once common. Sometimes we know the reasons, perhaps drainage of wet areas or the removal of trees and bushes where they once nested. But often the reasons are far from clear and research is needed to help us understand the changes and help to reverse them. Birds have many natural dangers, such as predators, bad weather and food shortages, but human activity has enormous impact. Very little of the British Isles is truly wild, but in recent years the changes have happened faster and are even more serious than before.

Marshland and fenland have been drained, chemicals are used on farmland, oil pollutes the sea, towns and roads spread even further into the countryside, trees are planted where once there were upland moors ... and so the catalogue of environmental damage continues.

Birds are often the first indicators of man's impact on the environment. It was the decline of the Peregrine and other birds of prey after World War II that warned us of the dangerous levels of chemicals being used in agriculture. More recently deaths of sea birds have shown us the levels of pollution in the sea.

It is in all our interests to ensure our birdlife is properly protected because a wide variety of birds indicates a healthy environment for other wildlife and for humans as well.

DIVERS AND GREBES

53–69 cm

J	F	M	A	M	J
J	A	S	O	N	D

Red-throated Diver
Gavia stellata

ID FACT FILE

SIZE: Mallard-sized

SUMMER: Velvet-grey head and neck, dark grey back, dull red throat

WINTER: Grey and white, pale around eye

BILL: Slender, pointed, upswept

IN FLIGHT: Hunch-backed, thin-necked

VOICE: Barking and wailing calls

LOOKALIKES: Black-throated Diver (p.10), Great Northern Diver (p.11), Cormorant (p.25)

Breeding on small freshwater lakes on open moorland in N Europe, this diver may fly to the sea to feed. It moves south to coastal waters in winter, and hunts fish by diving. The birds sometimes form loose flocks. The nest is a heap of vegetation at a traditional site close to the water's edge. The 2 eggs hatch after 27 days. Young leave the nest within a day, are fed by both parents and fly about 43 days later.

adult summer

adult winter

DIVERS AND GREBES

58–73 cm

J	F	M	A	M	J
J	A	S	O	N	D

ID FACT FILE

Size: Larger than Red-throated Diver

Summer: Grey head, black throat bordered with black and white stripes, white patches on back

Winter: Grey and white, dark cap to level of eye, pale thigh patch

Bill: Straight and pointed

In flight: Long and thin; longer legs than Red-throated Diver

Voice: Wailing call in spring

Lookalikes: Red-throated Diver (p.9), Great Northern Diver (p.11), Cormorant (p.25)

Black-throated Diver
Gavia arctica

This diver breeds on large freshwater lakes in open country or in forests, migrating south in autumn to coastal waters, or rarely inland. It can dive for up to 45 seconds to catch fish. Visits shorelines only to nest, and finds movement on land difficult. The birds sometimes gather in flocks. The nest is built on the ground close to the water's edge. The 2 eggs are incubated for 30 days. Young are cared for by both parents and fly after 65 days.

adult summer

adult winter

DIVERS AND GREBES

69–91 cm

J	F	M	A	M	J
J	A	S	O	N	D

Great Northern Diver
Gavia immer

ID FACT FILE

SIZE: Cormorant-sized

SUMMER: Thick neck with white collars, black head, black and white chequered back

WINTER: Grey and white

BILL: Strong, dagger-like

IN FLIGHT: Rather goose-like. Large feet trail behind tail

VOICE: Silent in winter. Wailing calls at breeding sites

LOOKALIKES: Black-throated Diver (p.10), Cormorant (p.25)

Breeds on large lakes in forest or on Arctic tundra in N America and Iceland, wintering in coastal waters in NW Europe, where a few remain all summer. It is unusual inland. The bird dives 4–10 m underwater for up to about a minute, feeding mainly on fish, but also on shellfish and crabs. It often rolls on its side to preen its white belly feathers. It runs along the surface of the water to take off. It is known as the Common Loon in N America.

adult summer

adult winter

27 cm

J	F	M	A	M	J
J	A	S	O	N	D

Little Grebe
Tachybaptus ruficollis

ID FACT FILE

SIZE: Smaller than Moorhen

SUMMER: Dark brown body, paler underparts, reddish-brown face and neck

WINTER: Paler brown and grey

YOUNG: Brown streaks on head

BILL: Short and pointed, yellow base in summer

IN FLIGHT: Reluctant to fly. No white patches in wings

VOICE: Loud trill

LOOKALIKES: Black-necked Grebe (p.16), Slavonian Grebe (p.15)

Small and secretive, the Little Grebe breeds on lakes, quiet rivers and small ponds in central and S Europe. There is some migration in spring and autumn. Sometimes the birds form flocks in winter. Dives when disturbed and when feeding. Food is insects and small fish. A floating nest of water weed is built among vegetation, and the 5 eggs hatch after 20 days. Young are cared for by both parents and often ride on their parents' backs. They fly after 46 days. There are 2 broods.

adult summer

adult winter

46–51 cm

Great Crested Grebe
Podiceps cristatus

ID FACT FILE

Size: Smaller than Mallard

Summer: Long white neck and white underparts, brown back, orange-brown crest and ear-tufts

Winter: Grey and white

Juvenile: Like winter adult. Stripy head and neck

Bill: Dagger-like

In flight: White patches on wings. Neck held out straight in front. Trailing feet

Voice: Low, growling

Lookalikes: Red-necked Grebe (p.14), Red-throated Diver (p.9)

Breeds on inland waters, but may be seen on the sea in winter and sometimes forms flocks. Northern grebes migrate south or west in autumn. Dives to find fish, and has elaborate courtship display. A floating nest is made of aquatic vegetation attached to water plants. The 3–5 eggs are incubated by both adults for 28 days. Young swim soon after hatching and ride on their parents' backs to protect them from predators such as pike. They fly after 71 days. There are 1 or 2 broods.

adult summer

adult winter

40–50 cm

| J | F | M | A | M | J |
| J | A | S | O | N | D |

Red-necked Grebe
Podiceps grisegena

ID FACT FILE

SIZE: Smaller than Mallard

SUMMER: Brown with reddish neck, white cheeks, black crown

WINTER: Grey and white, black crown to level of eye

BILL: Pointed, black with yellow base

IN FLIGHT: More compact than Great Crested Grebe. White wing-patches

VOICE: Trilling song in spring

LOOKALIKES: Great Crested Grebe (p.13), Slavonian Grebe (p.15)

Breeds inland on rather small and shallow lakes with reeds in parts of N and E Europe. Sometimes nests within colonies of gulls. After breeding the birds move south and west to open and often coastal waters. Dives to hunt aquatic insects and fish. The floating nest, made of aquatic vegetation, is attached to water plants. The 4–5 eggs hatch after 20 days. Young swim soon after hatching and fly after about 70 days.

adult winter

adult winter

adult summer

31–38 cm

J	F	M	A	M	J
J	A	S	O	N	D

Slavonian Grebe
Podiceps auritus

ID FACT FILE

Size: Similar to Moorhen

Summer: Chestnut flanks, breast and neck, black head with golden crest

Winter: Black and white, black cap, white behind eyes

Bill: Small, pointed, stubby

In flight: White trailing edge to wing, white shoulder patch

Voice: Squealing trill

Lookalikes: Black-necked Grebe (p.16), Red-necked Grebe (p.14)

This grebe breeds in sheltered bays of freshwater lakes in N Europe, moving south and west to coasts and large inland lakes in autumn. It dives to feed mainly on insects and their larvae in summer and small fish in winter. It nests among plants growing in water, sometimes in small colonies. The nest is a floating heap of weed, and 4 eggs are incubated for 24 days. Young ride on parents' backs soon after hatching and fly at 55 days.

adult summer

adult winter

28–34 cm

| J | F | M | A | M | J |
| J | A | S | O | N | D |

Black-necked Grebe
Podiceps nigricollis

ID FACT FILE

SIZE: Smaller than Moorhen

ALL BIRDS: Steep forehead

SUMMER: Black head, neck and upper parts, golden crest

WINTER: Black and white. Greyer cheeks and neck than Slavonian Grebe

BILL: Small, pointed and upswept

IN FLIGHT: Rapid wing-beats, white trailing edge

VOICE: Trill and piping calls in spring

LOOKALIKES: Slavonian Grebe (p.15), Little Grebe (p.12)

Breeding sites change frequently and include newly flooded areas. Small lakes with reeds and other vegetation are often chosen by small colonies, and the birds sometimes nest with a gull colony. They dive to feed on small fish, insects and shellfish. They visit larger lakes and coasts in winter. A floating nest of water weed is anchored to water plants. The 3–4 eggs hatch after 20 days. Young swim soon after hatching and ride on parents' backs when small.

adult summer

adult winter

SHEARWATERS AND PETRELS

45–50 cm

| J | F | M | A | M | J |
| A | S | O | N | D |

Fulmar
Fulmarus glacialis

ID FACT FILE

Size: Smaller than Herring Gull

All birds: White with greyish back, rump and tail, dark smudge round eye

Bill: Strong, stubby, tubed nostrils

In flight: Thick neck. Stiff-winged, shallow wing-beats. Frequently glides over waves

Voice: Cackling at nest-sites

Lookalikes: Herring Gull (p.132), Kittiwake (p.130)

A seabird, related to the albatrosses, which nests on cliffs and buildings near the sea in NW Europe. Fulmars are found all over the N Atlantic in winter, often feeding near fishing boats. They feed from the surface or plunge-dive for crustaceans, fish and offal. They breed after 6 years, nesting on narrow ledges with no nest material. One egg hatches after 50 days. The young bird is looked after by both parents and flies after 45 days.

adult

adult

45–53 cm

| J | F | M | A | M | J |
| J | A | S | O | N | D |

Cory's Shearwater

Calonectris diomedea

ID FACT FILE

SIZE: Smaller than Herring Gull

ALL BIRDS: Brown above, white below. Large head

BILL: Strong, long, pale, hooked at the tip

IN FLIGHT: Long-winged. Strong graceful flight, deep graceful flaps, low glides over the sea

VOICE: Silent at sea, rasping screech at nest sites

LOOKALIKES: Other shearwaters (pp.19–21)

This large shearwater spends most of its life in warm, open oceans and visits remote coasts and islands only to breed. Large flocks may form near breeding colonies or on migration. Feeds mainly at night on fish and offal from the surface or by shallow plunge-dives. Nests in colonies among boulders, in a chamber at the end of a tunnel. One egg hatches after 53 days, and the young bird flies after about 90 days.

adult

Breeds south of red line but ranges further afield

adult

adult

43–51 cm

J	F	M	A	M	J
J	A	S	O	N	D

Great Shearwater
Puffinus gravis

ID FACT FILE

Size: Larger than Manx Shearwater

All birds: Dark brown above, white below, dark cap, sometimes a pale collar, pale 'U'-shaped mark on rump

Bill: Long, dark, hooked tip

In flight: Powerful with rapid beats of stiff, long wings. Long glides, often close to the waves

Voice: Usually silent

Lookalikes: Other shearwaters (pp.18–21)

Breeding on remote islands in the S Atlantic, these shearwaters migrate northwards after nesting. The migration route brings them to W European coasts in late summer. They usually stay offshore in loose flocks. They are not afraid of ships and will associate with fishing boats and also with whales. The birds feed on fish and other marine life which they take from the surface or by shallow dives.

adult

adult

40–51 cm

J	F	M	A	M	J
J	A	S	O	N	D

ID FACT FILE

SIZE: Larger than Manx Shearwater

ALL BIRDS: Rather small head. Sooty brown all over except for white stripe under wing

BILL: Long, dark

IN FLIGHT: Long wings look narrow and swept back. Flight is swift on stiff wings

VOICE: Usually silent at sea

LOOKALIKES: Manx Shearwater (p.21)

Sooty Shearwater
Puffinus griseus

These shearwaters breed on islands off the coasts of S America, New Zealand and Australia, after which some move north into the Atlantic and reach European coastal waters. They feed on fish and other marine creatures, especially squid. Most food is taken from the surface, but the birds will also dive. Large flocks form in the Southern Ocean, but small numbers or single birds are more common in the N Atlantic.

adult

adults

30–38 cm

J	F	M	A	M	J
J	A	S	O	N	D

Manx Shearwater
Puffinus puffinus

ID FACT FILE

Size: Smaller than Herring Gull

All birds: Black above, white below, small head

Bill: Long, dark, hooked tip

In flight: Rapid, on stiff wings. Long glides close to the waves

Voice: Variety of howls and screams at burrows after dark

Lookalikes: Other shearwaters (pp.18–20)

A bird of the open ocean which comes ashore only to nest and then only after dark. It feeds out at sea on fish and other marine creatures which it takes from the surface or catches after shallow dives. Often seen from western headlands, especially in the evenings. The nests are in rabbit or Puffin burrows on islands, usually in large colonies. One egg hatches after 51 days. The young bird is abandoned by both parents after 60 days and leaves the burrow 8 or 9 days later.

adult

adult

SHEARWATERS AND PETRELS

14–18 cm

J	F	M	A	M	J
J	A	S	O	N	D

Storm Petrel
Hydrobates pelagicus

ID FACT FILE

SIZE: Sparrow-sized

ALL BIRDS: Black with white rump, and often with a white stripe under the wing

BILL: Small, black, hooked

IN FLIGHT: Weak, fluttering flight, sometimes with feet dangling

VOICE: Purring call heard only at the nest

LOOKALIKES: Leach's Petrel (p.23)

A tiny seabird of the open ocean which feeds on small sea-creatures and fish taken from the surface of the water. It often feeds in the wake of ships. Colonies nest in crevices between rocks close to the sea on rocky islands. The birds come to land at night during the breeding season. The single egg hatches after 40 days. The young bird is fed for 50 days before leaving for the open sea. Winters are spent off the African coast.

adult

adult
upperwing

adult
underwing

SHEARWATERS AND PETRELS

19–22 cm

J	F	M	A	M	J
J	A	S	O	N	D

Leach's Petrel
Oceanodroma leucorhoa

ID FACT FILE

SIZE: Larger than Storm Petrel

ALL BIRDS: Blackish, with dark mark down centre of white rump. Tail slightly forked, pale stripe on upper wings

BILL: Small, dark, hooked

IN FLIGHT: Jerky or dancing with changes of speed and direction. Longer wings than Storm Petrel

VOICE: Purring call at the nest

LOOKALIKES: Storm Petrel (p.22)

This secretive seabird breeds on remote rocky islands, but migrates to the tropics and sub-tropics in winter. It feeds on marine creatures taken from the surface, and comes to land only to breed and only at night. Sometimes in early autumn, many are blown off course and seen along western coasts, and even inland. Nests, which are in tunnels on islands, are often part of very large colonies. A single egg is incubated for 41 days, and the young can fly after 70 days.

adult

adult
upperwing

adult
underwing

87–100 cm

| J | F | M | A | M | J |
| J | A | S | O | N | D |

Gannet
Sula bassana

ID FACT FILE

Size: Larger than any gull

Adult: White, black wing-tips, yellow nape

Juvenile: Grey, gradually becoming white over 5 years

Bill: Dagger-like

In flight: Cigar-shaped with long, narrow, black-tipped wings

Voice: Usually silent, growling *urr* when nesting

Lookalikes: Skuas, Gulls and Terns (pp.123–139)

Birds of the open ocean, Gannets breed on small islands off the NW coast of Europe. They move away from land after nesting to winter at sea. The young migrate south as far as W Africa. Gannets feed on fish by plunge-diving from 25 m, and nest in large, noisy colonies. The nest is a pile of seaweed. A single egg is incubated for 44 days. The young bird is fed by both parents and flies after 90 days.

adults at breeding colony

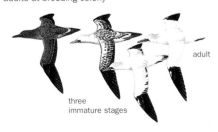

adult

three immature stages

80–100 cm

| J | F | M | A | M | J |
| J | A | S | O | N | D |

Cormorant
Phalacrocorax carbo

ID FACT FILE

SIZE: Like a large goose

BREEDING: Black, pale throat, white on back of head and on thighs

NON-BREEDING: Black, pale throat

JUVENILE: Dark brown upperparts, paler underparts darkening over first 2 years

BILL: Long, strong with hooked tip

IN FLIGHT: Goose-like with slow, strong wing-beats, neck held out in front

VOICE: Deep, guttural calls when nesting

LOOKALIKES: Shag (p.26), divers (pp.9–11)

Cormorants frequently stand with their wings partly spread. This is a mainly coastal bird, but it is also found along river valleys and on lakes far from the sea. It dives to feed on fish. Cormorants nest in colonies on cliff ledges, or sometimes in trees. The nest is made of twigs and seaweed. The 3–4 eggs hatch after 30 days and the young leave after 50 days, but may return to be fed for a further 50 days.

adult non-breeding

juvenile

immature

65–80 cm

J	F	M	A	M	J
J	A	S	O	N	D

Shag

Phalacrocorax aristotelis

ID FACT FILE

Size: Smaller and slimmer than Cormorant

Adult: Dark greenish-black, with forward-curling crest when breeding

Bill: Black with yellow base, finer than Cormorant's

Immature: Brown with paler under-parts

In flight: Low over water, neck outstretched. Rapid wing-beats

Voice: Clicks and grunts at nest

Lookalikes: Cormorant (p.25)

This is a marine species preferring rocky coasts and rarely coming inland. It dives to catch fish. Shags often stand with wings outstretched. They nest in well-spaced colonies on ledges or in caves just above the water-line. The nest is a heap of vegetation. The 1–6 eggs hatch after 30 days. Young leave the nest after 53 days, but may be cared for by parents for a further 50 days. Young breed after 3 or 4 years.

juvenile

adult

immature

70–80 cm

| J | F | M | A | M | J |
| J | A | S | O | N | D |

Bittern
Botaurus stellaris

ID FACT FILE

SIZE: Smaller than Grey Heron

ALL BIRDS: Stocky, thick-necked, golden-brown with black streaks and black crown

BILL: Long and dagger-like

IN FLIGHT: Broad, rounded wings. Neck hunched up and legs trailing

VOICE: Deep booming call of male in spring

LOOKALIKES: Grey Heron (p.29)

Secretive and solitary, this is a well-camouflaged bird of lowland marshes and dense reed-beds. It feeds mainly on fish, especially eels, but also eats other animals including small birds. Some northern Bitterns migrate in autumn. Males may have several mates. The nest is a heap of dead reeds. The 4–6 eggs hatch after 25 days. Young may leave the nest after 15 days and fly after 50 days.

adult

adult

adult

55–65 cm

| J | F | M | A | M | J |
| A | S | O | N | D |

Little Egret
Egretta garzetta

ID FACT FILE

Size: Smaller than Grey Heron

All birds: White, black legs, yellow feet

Bill: Long, pointed, black

In flight: Rounded wings, leisurely action, head hunched on shoulders, feet projecting beyond tail

Voice: Mostly silent

Lookalikes: None in area

A small white heron which catches fish and insects from the edges of lakes, slow-flowing rivers and estuaries. After nesting, young and adults disperse from the breeding areas before migrating. Some remain around the Mediterranean, but most fly to central Africa. In spring, some overshoot their normal breeding areas. Nests in colonies, laying 3–5 eggs which hatch after 21 days. Young leave the nest at 30 days and fly at about 40 days.

adult

adult

HERONS AND ALLIES

90–98 cm

| J | F | M | A | M | J |
| J | A | S | O | N | D |

ID FACT FILE

SIZE: Large, long necked, long-legged

ADULT: Grey and white with wispy black crest

JUVENILE: Greyer than adult and lacks crest

BILL: Long, dagger-like

IN FLIGHT: Slow, powerful wing-beats. Neck is drawn up on to shoulders, feet project beyond tail

VOICE: Harsh *frrank*

LOOKALIKES: None in area

Grey Heron
Ardea cinerea

This distinctive, large bird often stands beside water ready to grasp a passing fish, but may stand hunched up in a field away from water. It also feeds on amphibians or small mammals. Many European herons move south in autumn. Nests are in colonies (heronries) at the tops of tall trees. The nest is a large platform of sticks, in which 3–5 eggs are laid in February-April, hatching after 25 days. Young fly after 50 days and soon leave the area.

adult

immature

adult

HERONS AND ALLIES

80–90 cm

J	F	M	A	M	J
J	A	S	O	N	D

ID FACT FILE

Size: Smaller than Grey Heron

Adult: White, short crest, and yellowish band on breast when breeding

Juvenile: Black wing-tips. Lacks crest and yellow mark

Bill: Long and spoon-shaped

In flight: Neck held straight out in front, feet trailing

Voice: Usually silent. Bill snapping sometimes at nest

Lookalikes: None in area

Spoonbill
Platalea leucorodia

Coastal marshes and reed-beds in river valleys, mainly in SE Europe, are home for colonies of Spoonbills. They feed together in groups in open water, sweeping their bills from side to side as they filter the tiny creatures on which they feed. Most migrate away from colonies after nesting. The nest is a pile of reeds and twigs on the ground or in low trees or bushes. The 3–4 eggs are incubated for 24 days, and the young fly after about 24 days.

adult

adult

immature

SWANS, GEESE AND DUCKS

145–160 cm

| J | F | M | A | M | J |
| J | A | S | O | N | D |

Mute Swan
Cygnus olor

ID FACT FILE

SIZE: Very large with long neck

MALE: All white with prominent black knob at base of bill

FEMALE: As male, with smaller black knob

IMMATURE: Greyish-brown, with more white showing as it grows older

BILL: Orange-red with black marks

IN FLIGHT: Neck held out in front. Wings make loud rhythmic whistling

VOICE: Snorts and hisses

LOOKALIKES: Whooper Swan (p.33), Bewick's Swan (p.32)

A familiar bird of lakes and slow-flowing rivers, mainly in NW Europe. Most are resident, but north-easterly populations migrate south and west in autumn. Flocks of non-breeding, mainly young, birds may gather. Pairs nest singly. The large nest is made of rushes or reeds. The 5–8 eggs hatch after 36 days. Young swim soon after hatching and may ride on their parents' backs. Immatures may stay with the parents during their first winter.

adult

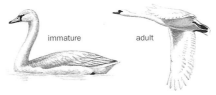

immature

adult

SWANS, GEESE AND DUCKS

115–127 cm

J	F	M	A	M	J
J	A	S	O	N	D

Bewick's Swan
Cygnus columbianus

ID FACT FILE

Size: Smaller than Mute Swan

Adults: White. Relatively short straight neck, domed head

Juvenile: Grey with pinkish bill

Bill: Black with varying amounts of yellow near base

In flight: Neck held out straight

Voice: Musical honking

Lookalikes: Mute Swan (p.31), Whooper Swan (p.33)

A winter visitor to W Europe from the flat, swampy Arctic tundra of Siberia where the breeding season is short. Family parties migrate together and usually stay together for the winter. They often join larger herds, which may number hundreds or even more at some traditional wintering grounds. Grazes on leaves, shoots and roots in flooded meadows, but also visits arable fields.

adult

juvenile

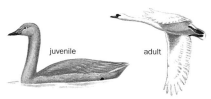

adult

145–160 cm

J	F	M	A	M	J
J	A	S	O	N	D

Whooper Swan
Cygnus cygnus

ID FACT FILE

SIZE: As Mute Swan

ADULT: White, sometimes with rust-coloured stains on neck. Base of long, straight neck often rests on back

JUVENILE: Brown with pink and black bill

BILL: Black with 'wedge' of yellow

IN FLIGHT: Neck held straight

VOICE: Trumpet-like call

LOOKALIKES: Mute Swan (p.31), Bewick's Swan (p.32)

This swan breeds in Iceland and parts of N Europe. It migrates southwards in autumn to lakes, rivers and sheltered coastal inlets. Family parties usually stay together and large flocks form where food is plentiful. Feeds mainly on aquatic vegetation, but also grazes on arable fields in winter. The nest is a large mound of vegetation into which 3–5 eggs are laid. Young hatch after 35 days and fly about 80 days later.

adult

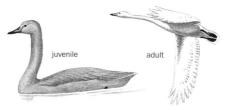

juvenile   adult

SWANS, GEESE AND DUCKS

66–84 cm

Bean Goose
Anser fabalis

ID FACT FILE

Size: Variable, slightly smaller than Greylag Goose

Adult: Slimmer than Greylag. Mostly brown with long dark neck, dark head, white at base of tail, orange legs

Juvenile: Duller, paler bill and legs

Bill: Orange-yellow and black, variable pattern

In flight: Long, dark neck. Darker wings than Greylag

Voice: Muffled barking

Lookalikes: Greylag Goose (p.37), Pink-footed Goose (p.35), White-fronted Goose (p.36)

In its northern breeding grounds this goose is unique in that some birds nest in dense coniferous or birch forests. Elsewhere the birds nest in more open locations including Arctic tundra. For many parts of Europe this is a winter migrant and small flocks visit fields, river valleys and sometimes coastal marshes with only a few reaching the British Isles. It grazes on grasses, seeds, roots and even berries. Family parties stay together for most of the winter.

adult

juvenile

adult

SWANS, GEESE AND DUCKS

60–75 cm

J	F	M	A	M	J
J	A	S	O	N	D

Pink-footed Goose
Anser brachyrhynchus

ID FACT FILE

Size: Smaller than Greylag Goose

Adult: Medium-sized pinkish goose with rather short, dark neck and rounded head

Juvenile: Darker and more mottled

Bill: Variable pink and black pattern

In flight: Faster and daintier, with shorter neck and paler forewings than Greylag Goose

Voice: Soft *wink-wink*

Lookalikes: Greylag Goose (p.37), Bean Goose (p.34), White-fronted Goose (p.36)

This goose breeds on the ground in remote parts of Iceland, Greenland and Spitsbergen. Large flocks winter together in Britain, Ireland and other countries bordering the North Sea. They roost on estuaries, but also on freshwater lakes and sometimes on heather moors. They feed on vegetable matter growing above or below the ground. The young migrate with their parents and stay with them through the first winter and on the return migration.

adult

juvenile

adult

65–78 cm

| J | F | M | A | M | J |
| J | A | S | O | N | D |

ID FACT FILE

Size: Smaller than Greylag Goose

Adult: Deep chest and squarish head. Grey-brown, white forehead; black bars on belly

Juvenile: No white on face or black bars on belly

Bill: Orange or pink

In flight: Squarish head, deep chest, often very agile

Voice: More high-pitched than other grey geese

Lookalikes: Bean Goose (p.34), Pink-footed Goose (p.35), Greylag Goose (p.37)

White-fronted Goose
Anser albifrons

In winter this is the most numerous goose in Europe. It breeds on the Arctic tundra and migrates in autumn. Most European migrants come from Arctic Russia but some from Greenland winter in the British Isles, especially in Ireland. Feeds on leaves, roots and seeds. Young stay with their parents for the first autumn and winter and families often start the return migration together.

adult

juvenile

adult

75–90 cm

| J | F | M | A | M | J |
| J | A | S | O | N | D |

Greylag Goose
Anser anser

ID FACT FILE

SIZE: The largest brown goose

ALL BIRDS: Brown, with thick, pale neck and large, pale head

BILL: Strong, triangular. Orange on western birds, pink on eastern populations

IN FLIGHT: Heavy-looking, with large head, thick neck, blue-grey patches on wings

VOICE: Deep honking calls

LOOKALIKES: Bean Goose (p.34), Pink-footed Goose (p.35), White-fronted Goose (p.36)

The Greylag is the ancestor of many domesticated geese. It breeds in N and E European wetlands, from Arctic tundra to reed-beds. In autumn it migrates south and west to traditional wintering areas. It feeds on plant material, and lays 4–6 eggs in a nest of locally gathered vegetation. Young hatch after 27 days, fly about 50 days later and stay with their parents for the first autumn and winter.

adult

juvenile

adult

SWANS, GEESE AND DUCKS

58–70 cm

| J | F | M | A | M | J |
| J | A | S | O | N | D |

ID FACT FILE

SIZE: Smaller than Canada Goose

ADULT: Black and grey with white face and barred back

JUVENILE: Similar to adult but duller, with some brown feathers and a black line through the eye

BILL: Small and black

IN FLIGHT: Looks black and white, with a longish neck and rather pointed wings

VOICE: Dog-like yelping

LOOKALIKES: Canada Goose (p.40), Brent Goose (p.39)

Barnacle Goose
Branta leucopsis

Barnacle Geese breed in the Arctic on steep cliffs and rock pinnacles or hummocks on lower ground. There are 3 separate populations, in Greenland, Spitsbergen and Novaya Zemlya, and all have separate migration routes and different wintering areas: the Novaya Zemlya population winters in the Netherlands, the others in the British Isles. They eat grasses and other vegetation. Young stay with their parents for the first autumn and winter.

adult

juvenile

adult

SWANS, GEESE AND DUCKS

51–61 cm

J	F	M	A	M	J
J	A	S	O	N	D

Brent Goose
Branta bernicla

ID FACT FILE

SIZE: Small, Mallard-sized goose

ADULT: Small black head, white patch on side of black neck, dark brown body.

SIBERIAN BIRDS: Dark belly

GREENLAND BIRDS: Pale belly

JUVENILE: Like adult without neck patch, and with more barring on back

BILL: Short and black

IN FLIGHT: Fast, with rather pointed wings and short neck

VOICE: Flocks have murmuring, growling calls

LOOKALIKES: Barnacle Goose (p.38)

These geese breed on the low tundra of the Arctic. Breeding must take place within 100 days before snow and ice return. Two populations winter in Europe: Siberian birds migrate across NW Europe to winter in the Netherlands, France and England; others from Greenland fly to Ireland with a few reaching Britain and France. In winter they feed on vegetation growing around coast and in estuaries, but also in arable fields near the sea.

adult dark-bellied

juvenile dark-bellied

adult

SWANS, GEESE AND DUCKS

56–110 cm

J	F	M	A	M	J
J	A	S	O	N	D

Canada Goose
Branta canadensis

ID FACT FILE

Size: The largest goose in Europe, but different races vary in size

All birds: Brown body, black neck and head, white chin patch

Bill: Large and black

In flight: Fast, with deep, regular wing-beats

Voice: Loud honking

Lookalikes: Barnacle Goose (p.38), Brent Goose (p.39)

Introduced from N America, the Canada Goose now breeds widely in the British Isles and parts of Scandinavia, but some genuinely wild birds may reach Europe from time to time. It feeds on plants and favours lowland lakes. There is some local migration. The nest is a pile of grass and leaves near water. The 5–6 eggs hatch after 28 days and young fly after 40 days. Families stay together for the first winter.

adult

juvenile

adult

63–73 cm

J	F	M	A	M	J
J	A	S	O	N	D

ID FACT FILE

Size: Larger than Shelduck

Adult: Long neck and legs. Grey-brown with darker back, dark patch round eye, dark spot on breast

Juvenile: Darker head. Lacks dark patches round eye and on breast

Bill: Heavy-looking, pink and black

In flight: Large white patches on wings

Voice: Husky puffing and louder trumpeting

Lookalikes: Grey geese (pp.34–37), Shelduck (p.42)

Egyptian Goose
Alopochen aegyptiacus

Introduced to E England from Africa, these geese now breed wild in parkland and near some lowland lakes. Feeds mainly on leaves, grasses and seeds. Nests on a mound of leaves and reeds, laying 8 or 9 eggs which hatch after 28 days. Young feed themselves and are cared for by both parents. They fly after about 75 days.

adult

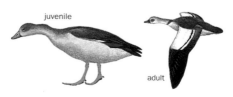

juvenile

adult

58–67 cm

J	F	M	A	M	J
J	A	S	O	N	D

Shelduck
Tadorna tadorna

ID FACT FILE

Size: Larger than Mallard

Adult: Black and white with dark green head and orange band on breast

Juvenile: Grey-brown above, white below and pale face

Bill: Red. Male's has enlarged knob at base

In flight: Black and white, rather goose-like

Voice: Growling *ark-ark-ark*

Lookalikes: Shoveler (p.50), Eider (p.55), Goosander (p.60), Red-breasted Merganser (p.61)

This is mainly a coastal species but sometimes breeds inland. Most live on estuaries or muddy shores where they filter molluscs, crustaceans and other invertebrates from the mud. Nests in enclosed sites such as rabbit burrows. Lays 8–10 eggs, which hatch after 29 days. The young join other broods and parents often leave them with an 'auntie' and migrate to a special moulting area. Young are independent at 20 days and able to fly after 45 days.

adult male

juvenile

adult

41–49 cm

Mandarin
Aix galericulata

ID FACT FILE

SIZE: Smaller than Mallard

MALE: Striking, with crest, large white eye-stripe, multi-coloured plumage, orange neck feathers and 'sails' on its back

FEMALE: Grey-brown with spotted sides and pale 'spectacles'

ECLIPSE: May–Sep. Male similar to female with reddish bill

BILL: Male red, female purple

IN FLIGHT: Small and agile with pale belly

VOICE: Usually silent; whistles and snorts during courtship

LOOKALIKES: None in area

A spectacular duck introduced from the Far East and now breeding in many locations in Britain where there are lakes, mature trees, a supply of insect food in summer and nuts in autumn. Nests in holes, usually high in oak trees. The 9–12 eggs hatch after 28 days and young fly after 40 days. Unlike other ducks pairs remain faithful and the male stays with the family in summer. Asian birds migrate but no migration of British birds has been recorded.

adult male

adult female

adult female

adult male

SWANS, GEESE AND DUCKS

45–51 cm

| J | F | M | A | M | J |
| J | A | S | O | N | D |

Wigeon
Anas penelope

ID FACT FILE

SIZE: Smaller than Mallard

MALE: Chestnut head with yellow crown. Grey body with pale pink breast, white wing-patches

FEMALE: Mottled brown, rounded crown

ECLIPSE: Jun–Oct. Male like female with white wing-patches

JUVENILE: First-winter males lack wing-patches

BILL: Rather small

IN FLIGHT: Pale belly, long, narrow wings

VOICE: Loud *we-ooo*

LOOKALIKES: Pochard (p.52), Teal (p.46), Gadwall (p.45), Mallard (p.47)

The Wigeon is more likely than other ducks to be seen out of the water grazing on grass. A winter visitor to most of Europe, mainly to coastal areas, it will also follow river valleys to inland lakes and flooded fields. It feeds on leaves, stems and seeds, and nests among vegetation near lakes in N Europe. The 8 or 9 eggs hatch after 24 days. Young feed themselves and fly after about 40 days.

adult male

adult female

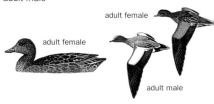

adult female

adult male

SWANS, GEESE AND DUCKS

46–56 cm

| J | F | M | A | M | J |
| J | A | S | O | N | D |

Gadwall
Anas strepera

ID FACT FILE

Size: Smaller than Mallard

Male: Finely marked grey body, black tail

Female: Mallard-like but more graceful, with white wing-patch

Eclipse: May–Sep. Male like female but a little greyer

Bill: Male's is grey, female's has orange sides

In flight: White wing-patch on both male and female

Voice: Male has croaking call, female a quiet quack

Lookalikes: Mallard (p.47), Pintail (p.48), Pochard (p.52)

A delicately marked duck which breeds in scattered locations in many parts of Europe and winters in others. Feeds mainly on water plants. Nests close to lowland lakes with plenty of vegetation. Moves to larger lakes in winter and is joined by migrants from the north-east. The 8–12 eggs hatch after 24 days. Young are looked after by the female and can feed themselves. They fly after 45 days.

adult male

adult female

adult female

adult male

SWANS, GEESE AND DUCKS

34–38 cm

J	F	M	A	M	J
J	A	S	O	N	D

Teal
Anas crecca

ID FACT FILE

Size: Smaller than Mallard

Male: Chestnut and green head, white stripe along grey body, yellow patch under tail

Female: Like small female Mallard with green speculum

Eclipse: Jun–Sep. Male resembles dark female

Bill: Small and grey

In flight: Rapid, often twisting like waders

Voice: Piping

Lookalikes: Garganey (p.49)

The smallest and most secretive European duck breeds in wetlands throughout N Europe and in a few southerly locations. Autumn migration takes it to many more freshwater and coastal marshes for the winter. Feeds on seeds and small creatures which it filters from the water or from soft mud. Nests under cover near water. Egg-laying starts in mid-April, and 8–11 eggs hatch after 21 days. Young feed themselves and fly after about 25 days.

adult male

adult female

adult female

adult male

SWANS, GEESE AND DUCKS

50–65 cm

| J | F | M | A | M | J |
| J | A | S | O | N | D |

Mallard
Anas platyrhynchos

ID FACT FILE

Size: The largest common duck

Male: Green head, grey body, purple-brown breast

Female: Mottled brown

Eclipse: Jul–Sep. Male like female with dark crown and yellow bill

Bill: Large. Male's yellow, female's horn-coloured

In flight: Blue speculum

Voice: Female quacks, male has quieter *arrk*

Lookalikes: Other ducks (pp.42–63)

The most widespread duck in the world and familiar on park lakes as well as in remote wetlands throughout Europe. Northern populations migrate south and west in winter. Feeds on a variety of animal and vegetable material. Usually nests under cover, but may nest off the ground in trees. Egg-laying starts in March, and 9–13 eggs take 27 days to hatch. Young feed themselves and dive to escape danger. They fly after about 50 days.

adult male

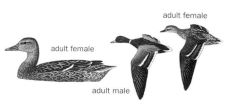

adult female

adult female

adult male

51–66 cm

| J | F | M | A | M | J |
| J | A | S | O | N | D |

ID FACT FILE

Size: Mallard-sized with longer neck

Male: Grey body, long pointed tail, creamy breast and brown head with white stripe on neck

Female: Mallard-like, greyer, with longer neck

Eclipse: Jul–Oct. Male like female, but with darker upperparts

Bill: Grey

In flight: Long neck and tail

Voice: Like quiet Mallard

Lookalikes: Other dabbling ducks (pp.44–50)

Pintail
Anas acuta

This elegant, long-necked duck breeds near open, fresh water in N and E Europe, and sporadically farther south. In autumn migrants fly south and west mainly to coastal wetlands, especially estuaries. Pintails feed on a variety of plant and animal matter. Nests may be several hundred kilometres from water among grasses or rushes, and 7–9 eggs, laid in April and May, hatch after 22 days. Young feed themselves and fly after about 40 days.

adult male

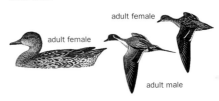

adult female

adult female

adult male

SWANS, GEESE AND DUCKS

37–41 cm

| J | F | M | A | M | J |
| J | A | S | O | N | D |

Garganey
Anas querquedula

ID FACT FILE

SIZE: Smaller than Mallard

MALE: Large white stripe over eye and elongated feathers on back

FEMALE: Like female Teal with dark eye-stripe and pale stripe above eye

ECLIPSE: Jul–Sep. Male resembles female with brighter blue on wings

BILL: Grey

IN FLIGHT: Blue-grey forewing, female's duller than male's

VOICE: Mechanical-sounding rattle

LOOKALIKES: Teal (p.46)

A small duck which is fully migratory, a summer visitor to parts of Europe from Africa. Nests among thick vegetation close to inland pools of shallow, fresh water with lots of emergent water plants. Feeds on insects and also buds, leaves, roots and seeds. Lays 8–9 eggs which hatch after 21 days. Young feed themselves and fly after 35–40 days.

adult male

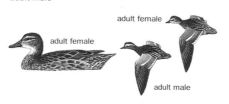

adult female

adult female

adult male

SWANS, GEESE AND DUCKS

44–52 cm

Shoveler
Anas clypeata

The Shoveler uses its large, broad bill to filter small creatures and seeds from the water and mud. Shovelers nest near shallow inland waters with lots of vegetation. In winter they migrate south to similar habitats. In the British Isles most Shovelers migrate south, but are replaced by migrants from the north-east. The 9–11 eggs hatch after 22 days. Young are cared for by the female, feed themselves and fly after 40 days.

ID FACT FILE

SIZE: Similar to Mallard

MALE: Green head, white breast and orange sides

FEMALE: Mallard-like, with green speculum

ECLIPSE: May–Sep, male is like female; Sep–Nov, male has scaly-looking breeding lumage

BILL: Very large and broad

IN FLIGHT: Wings set far back; blue forewings

VOICE: Hoarse *took, took*

LOOKALIKES: Mallard (p.47)

adult male

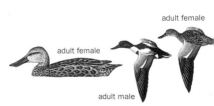

adult female

adult female

adult male

adult male

53–57 cm

J	F	M	A	M	J
J	A	S	O	N	D

Red-crested Pochard
Netta rufina

ID FACT FILE

Size: Similar to Mallard

Male: Orange head and crest, black neck and breast, pale sides

Female: Brown, with pale cheeks and dark crown

Eclipse: May–Oct. Male resembles female but with red bill and larger head

Bill: Male's is bright red, female's grey

In flight: White wing-bar and white belly

Voice: Usually silent

Lookalikes: Pochard (p.52)

A diving duck with a long neck and a large, rounded head. At home around inland lakes in Asia, in Europe it breeds in only a few scattered locations, often on smaller waters surrounded by reeds and other vegetation. A partial migrant and a frequent escapee from collections. Feeds on water plants by diving or up-ending. The 8–10 eggs hatch after 26 days. Young feed themselves and fly after 45 days.

adult male

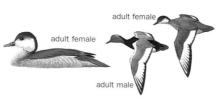

adult female

adult female

adult male

42–49 cm

J	F	M	A	M	J
J	A	S	O	N	D

Pochard
Aythya ferina

ID FACT FILE

SIZE: Smaller than Mallard

MALE: Reddish-brown head, grey body, black breast and tail

FEMALE: Grey-brown body, blotchy cheeks

ECLIPSE: Jul–Aug. Male resembles female but greyer

BILL: Grey with silvery band

IN FLIGHT: Pale body contrasts with black breast and tail

VOICE: Usually silent, but wings make whistling sound

LOOKALIKES: Wigeon (p.44), Tufted Duck (p.53)

A diving duck which breeds around inland lakes in many parts of Europe and reaches others as a winter migrant, when it often gathers in large flocks. It mostly feeds on plants that grow on the bottom of shallow lakes, which it reaches by diving. It nests in dense cover close to water. The 8–10 eggs hatch after 25 days. Young are cared for by the female, feed themselves and fly after 50 days.

adult male

adult female

adult female

adult male

40–47 cm

| J | F | M | A | M | J |
| J | A | S | O | N | D |

ID FACT FILE

Size: Smaller than Mallard

Male: Black with white sides. Black drooping crest

Female: Dark brown with pale brown sides

Eclipse: Jul–Oct. Male resembles female with darker upper-parts and paler under-parts

Bill: Grey

In flight: White wing-bar, white belly on male

Voice: Variety of quiet calls

Lookalikes: Scaup (p.54), Goldeneye (p.59), Common Scoter (p.57)

Tufted Duck
Aythya fuligula

This diving duck breeds across N Europe and in some southerly locations. In autumn it migrates south and west to both inland and coastal areas. It feeds on water plants, invertebrates and especially freshwater mussels, diving up to 14 m to take food from the bottom of lakes. It nests near water and lays 8–11 eggs. Young hatch after 25 days and feed on midge larvae. They fly after 45 days.

adult male

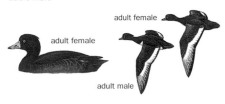

adult female

adult female

adult male

42–51 cm

Scaup
Aythya marila

A diving duck which breeds further north than other members of its family, migrating to mainly northern coastal waters for the winter. It feeds on a variety of food including mussels which it picks off the sea-bed. Most feeding takes place at night. The nest is on the ground among grasses or rushes near water. The 8–11 eggs hatch after 26 days. Young feed themselves and fly about 40 days later.

ID FACT FILE

SIZE: Smaller than Mallard

MALE: Black head, breast and tail, white sides and grey back

FEMALE: Brown. Large pale patch at base of bill

ECLIPSE: Jul–Nov. Male becomes duller

BILL: Grey-blue

IN FLIGHT: Broad white wing-bar

VOICE: Usually silent

LOOKALIKES: Tufted Duck (p.53), Goldeneye (p.59)

adult male

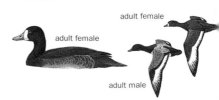

adult female

adult female

adult male

50–71 cm

J	F	M	A	M	J
J	A	S	O	N	D

Eider
Somateria mollissima

ID FACT FILE

SIZE: As Mallard

MALE: Black and white, with lime-green nape

FEMALE: Dark, mottled brown

ECLIPSE: Jul–Sep. Male sooty-brown; forewings white

JUVENILE: Young males have a variety of black-and-white plumages

BILL: Large, wedge-shaped

IN FLIGHT: Male black behind, white in front; female brown and heavy-looking

VOICE: Cooing calls in spring

LOOKALIKES: Long-tailed Duck (p.56), Goldeneye (p.59), Goosander (p.60), Shelduck (p.42)

This marine diving duck breeds around rocky coasts of N Europe and winters only a little farther south. It tears mussels from rocks with its strong bill. The nest of down from the female's breast may be in the open or sheltered by rocks. The 4–6 eggs hatch after 25 days. Young feed themselves. While parents moult, creches of young are cared for by 'aunties'. Young fly after 65 days.

adult male

adult female

adult male

adult female

adult female

adult male eclipse

SWANS, GEESE AND DUCKS

40–47 cm

J	F	M	A	M	J
J	A	S	O	N	D

Long-tailed Duck
Clangula hyemalis

ID FACT FILE

SIZE: Smaller than Mallard

MALE (SUMMER): Brown, white sides, white face

MALE (WINTER): Black and white, black cheek

FEMALE: Brown body, pale face, dark smudge on cheeks

ECLIPSE: Jul–Aug. Male in dull summer plumage

BILL: pink and black

IN FLIGHT: White body, dark wings

VOICE: Cooing *ah-oo-ah*

LOOKALIKES: Pintail (p.48), Eider (p.55), Goldeneye (p.59), Smew (p.62)

This duck breeds on islands or among vegetation near small tundra pools in the high Arctic, and is a winter visitor to coasts of NW Europe. The male is unusual in having 3 distinct plumages each year. The ducks feed on crabs and shellfish which they catch underwater, laying 6–9 eggs which hatch after 24 days. Young feed themselves, although food may be stirred up by the female. They fly after about 35 days.

adult male winter

adult male summer

adult female summer

adult male winter

adult female winter

SWANS, GEESE AND DUCKS

44–54 cm

| J | F | M | A | M | J |
| J | A | S | O | N | D |

ID FACT FILE

Size: Smaller than Mallard

Male: All black

Female: Dark brown with pale cheeks and neck

Bill: Male's yellow with knob at base, female's grey

In flight: All black, flies low over waves

Voice: Various whistles and piping calls

Lookalikes: Velvet Scoter (p.58)

Common Scoter
Melanitta nigra

Despite belonging to a group whose members are often called sea ducks, the Common Scoter frequently nests among vegetation on the Arctic tundra, far from the sea. In winter, though, it lives up to its reputation and flocks to inshore waters along the Atlantic coasts. It feeds mainly on molluscs which it finds by diving. It lays 6–8 eggs. Young hatch after 30 days and fly after about 45 days.

adult male

adult female

adult female

adult male

SWANS, GEESE AND DUCKS

51–58 cm

| J | F | M | A | M | J |
| J | A | S | O | N | D |

Velvet Scoter
Melanitta fusca

ID FACT FILE

Size: As Mallard

Male: Black with white wing-patch

Female: Brown with white wing-patch and pale patches on head

Bill: Male's yellow and black with knob at base; female's grey

In flight: Black with white wing-patch

Voice: Low growling, sometimes piping

Lookalikes: Common Scoter (p.57)

This 'sea duck' breeds further from the sea than the Common Scoter, and even nests in areas with trees. Winters off the coasts of NW Europe, but also visits large inland lakes. At sea it may join flocks of Common Scoter. Dives to search for molluscs. The 7–9 eggs hatch after 27 days. Young feed themselves and fly after 50 days. In July flocks gather off the coast of Denmark to moult.

adult male

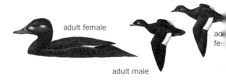

adult female

adult male

adult female

42–50 cm

J	F	M	A	M	J
J	A	S	O	N	D

Goldeneye
Bucephala clangula

ID FACT FILE

Size: Smaller than Mallard

Male: White with dark head and back. White spot in front of eye

Eclipse: Aug–Sep, Male resembles female

Female: Grey with brown head, white collar, white in wings

Bill: Rather small and dark

In flight: Wings whistle. White wing-patches

Voice: Usually silent. Low growls during courtship

Lookalikes: Long-tailed Duck (p.56), Smew (p.62), Eider (p.55), Tufted Duck (p.53)

A large-headed diving duck which nests in northern coniferous forests where there are lakes or rivers. Nests in holes in trees and will use special nestboxes. Migrates south and west in winter and visits inland lakes and the coast. Feeds on molluscs, crustaceans and insect larvae. The 8–11 eggs hatch after 29 days. Young feed themselves and are brooded by female. They fly after about 57 days.

adult male

adult female

adult male

adult female

58–66 cm

| J | F | M | A | M | J |
| J | A | S | O | N | D |

ID FACT FILE

Size: Larger than Mallard

Male: White with large green head and black back

Female: Grey body, drooping crest; contrast between reddish head, white throat and grey neck

Eclipse and Juvenile: Similar to female

Bill: Long and thin

In flight: White wing-patches (male's larger than female's)

Voice: Hoarse *kar-r-r*

Lookalikes: Red-breasted Merganser (p.61), Great Crested Grebe (p.13), Eider (p.55)

Goosander
Mergus merganser

The largest 'sawbill' which breeds near northern lakes and rivers. It migrates to more southerly lakes in winter and visits coastal waters less frequently than the Red-breasted Merganser. It will nest in crevices on the ground, but more often in holes in trees or nestboxes. Feeds on fish which it catches by diving. The 8–11 eggs hatch after 30 days. Young feed themselves and may join with other family groups. They fly after 60–70 days.

adult male

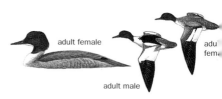

adult female

adult male

adult female

SWANS, GEESE AND DUCKS

52–58 cm

J	F	M	A	M	J
J	A	S	O	N	D

ID FACT FILE

Size: Similar to Mallard

Male: Green head, wispy crest, grey body, chestnut breast

Female: Grey with reddish head merging with pale throat and grey neck

Eclipse and Juvenile: Similar to female

Bill: Long, thin

In flight: White wing-patches, male's crossed by black bars

Voice: Harsh *kar-r-r*

Lookalikes: Goosander (p.60), Great Crested Grebe (p.13)

Red-breasted Merganser
Mergus serrator

Swims with head submerged before diving to pursue fish underwater. A group of these 'saw-bills' will hunt cooperatively by swimming in lines and driving fish into shallow water. Breeds near fresh or salt water and winters in coastal areas. Nests on the ground amongst vegetation or in a crevice, often in or near woodland. Lays 8–10 eggs which hatch after 31 days. Young feed themselves and broods often merge together. Young fledge after 60 days.

adult male

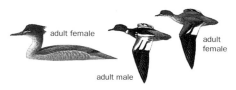

adult female

adult male

adult female

38–44 cm

Smew
Mergus albellus

ID FACT FILE

Size: Smaller than Mallard

Male: White with black marks. Small crest

Female and juvenile: Grey. Reddish-brown head, white throat and neck

Bill: Small, dark grey

In flight: Black and white wing-pattern. Male has white body

Voice: Usually silent

Lookalikes: Goldeneye (p.59), Goosander (p.60), Red-breasted Merganser (p.61)

This smallest member of the Merganser family is an attractive diving duck and a winter visitor from northern forests to inland lakes in central and S Europe. Females and juveniles, collectively known as redheads, migrate further south than males. In some winters large concentrations occur in the Netherlands. It feeds on fish and insects which it catches by diving. In its summer home it nests in holes in trees and will use nestboxes.

adult male

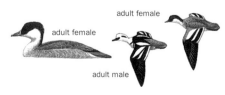

adult female

adult female

adult male

SWANS, GEESE AND DUCKS

35–43 cm

| J | F | M | A | M | J |
| J | A | S | O | N | D |

Ruddy Duck
Oxyura jamaicensis

ID FACT FILE

SIZE: Smaller than Mallard

MALE: Reddish-brown with white face

FEMALE: Brown with pale cheeks. Dark line under eye

ECLIPSE: Male similar to female with paler cheeks

BILL: Large. Male's blue, female's grey

IN FLIGHT: Rapid. No distinctive marks on wings

VOICE: Bill rattling and chest-beating produce hollow, non vocal sounds during display

LOOKALIKES: None

A small N American duck belonging to the 'stiff-tail' family. Brought to Europe for wildfowl collections. Many have been released or escaped and a wild population now lives in Britain. Some have moved to Continental Europe where they hybridise with the endangered White-headed Duck. Dives to feed on insects and water plants. Nest built among vegetation growing in water. Lays 6–10 eggs which hatch after 25 days. Young feed themselves and fly after about 50 days.

adult male

adult female

adult female

male eclipse

adult male

BIRDS OF PREY

55–58 cm

J	F	M	A	M	J
J	A	S	O	N	D

Osprey
Pandion haliaetus

ID FACT FILE

Size: Slightly larger than Buzzard

Adults: Dark brown above, white below with dark marks. White head with dark mask

Juvenile: Spotted back

Bill: Hooked and dark

In flight: Long wings, dark 'elbows', wings often bowed

Voice: High-pitched whistles heard at nest

Lookalikes: Buzzard (p.69), Honey Buzzard (p.67)

Ospreys visit every continent except Antarctica. They are migrants, returning to Europe from Africa each spring. They usually nest in trees but will use cliffs. They need a regular supply of fish which they catch during spectacular, feet-first dives into lakes, rivers or the sea. The nest is a large structure of sticks which is re-used year after year. The 2 or 3 eggs hatch after 37 days and the young fly 53 days later.

adult

adult

adult (from below)

BIRDS OF PREY

70–90 cm

| J | F | M | A | M | J |
| J | A | S | O | N | D |

White-tailed Eagle (Sea Eagle)

Haliaeetus albicilla

ID FACT FILE

SIZE: The largest European eagle

ADULTS: Brown with pale head and white tail

JUVENILE: Dark, spotted. Pale line on under-wing

BILL: Huge, hooked

IN FLIGHT: Broad, rectangular, fingered wings and short, wedge-shaped tail. Shallow wing-beats and shallow, long glides

VOICE: Yelping *kyick, kyick*

LOOKALIKES: Golden Eagle (p.66)

This huge eagle nests on cliffs, in trees or sometimes on the ground in N and E Europe. It was recently reintroduced to Scotland. It breeds near coasts, large rivers and lakes. Some birds migrate to central and S Europe. Feeds on fish, birds, mammals and carrion. Usually lays 2 eggs which hatch after 38 days. The young are cared for by both parents, fly after 70 days and are fed by parents for a further 35 days. Juveniles flock in winter.

adult

adult
(from below)

juvenile
(from below)

BIRDS OF PREY

75–88 cm

J	F	M	A	M	J
J	A	S	O	N	D

Golden Eagle
Aquila chrysaetos

ID FACT FILE

SIZE: Much larger than Buzzard

ADULT: All dark with yellow-brown head

JUVENILE: Dark, with pale panel along centre of wing and white base to tail

BILL: Hooked, strong

IN FLIGHT: Wings held in shallow 'V' when soaring or gliding

VOICE: Yelping calls

LOOKALIKES: White-tailed Eagle (p.65)

Persecution has restricted this huge eagle to large mountain ranges and some remote forests. It is mainly resident, but young wander from their breeding sites. It eats medium-sized mammals and birds. The nest is a large structure of branches on cliff faces or in trees. Generally 2 eggs are laid but often only 1 young is reared. Eggs take 43 days to hatch, young fly after 65 days and are fed by parents for a further 3 months.

adult

adult
(from below)

juvenile
(from below)

BIRDS OF PREY

52–60 cm

| J | F | M | A | M | J |
| J | A | S | O | N | D |

Honey Buzzard
Pernis apivorus

ID FACT FILE

SIZE: Slightly larger than Buzzard

ADULT: Small head and neck, long tail, variable colour

JUVENILE: Dark, lacking adult pattern. Dark trailing edge to wing

BILL: Small, cuckoo-like

IN FLIGHT: Light or dark, with 3 dark bands on wings and tail, and black projecting 'elbows'

VOICE: Drawn-out *wh-ee-oo*

LOOKALIKES: Buzzard (p.69), Goshawk (p.74),

A summer migrant to European woodland which feeds on nests and larvae of wasps and bees. It winters in Africa, returning in April and leaving again by September. Nests in trees, using an old crow's or Buzzard's nest or building its own of twigs and green leaves. Lays 2 eggs which hatch after 30 days. Young fly 40 days later, return to the nest for a further 15 days and are then independent after approximately a month.

adult

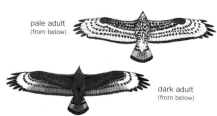

pale adult
(from below)

dark adult
(from below)

BIRDS OF PREY

60–66 cm

| J | F | M | A | M | J |
| J | A | S | O | N | D |

Red Kite

Milvus milvus

ID FACT FILE

SIZE: Larger than Buzzard

ADULT: Rusty-red with pale head

JUVENILE: Similar to adult but with more spotted back and less contrasting underparts

BILL: Hooked, quite small

IN FLIGHT: Very manoeuvrable. Long forked tail, long narrow wings, large pale patch at base of flight feathers

VOICE: Wailing *heh, he, he, he, heh*

LOOKALIKES: Buzzard (p.69)

An elegant bird of prey which catches some live prey, but often eats carrion. It was once familiar in much of Europe, but persecution and food shortage now restrict it to more remote uplands and secluded valleys. It is mainly migratory in the north, and is seen in numbers around winter food supplies. The nest is in the fork of a tree. The 1–3 eggs hatch after 31 days. Young fly at 50–70 days, but are fed by parents for another 20 days or more.

adult

adult
(from below)

BIRDS OF PREY

51–57 cm

| J | F | M | A | M | J |
| A | S | O | N | D |

Buzzard
Buteo buteo

ID FACT FILE

Size: Larger than Carrion Crow

All birds: Variable. Brown back, paler underparts; may have pale crescent on breast

Bill: Hooked

In flight: Broad, rounded wings, short neck, shortish tail, pale patch at base of flight feathers

Voice: Mewing call

Lookalikes: Honey Buzzard (p.67), Golden Eagle (p.66), Goshawk (p.74)

Buzzards leave N and E Europe each autumn, elsewhere they are mainly resident. They live in cultivated country and also in uplands with wooded valleys. They feed on small mammals and other animals. Wings are held in a shallow 'V' when soaring, and the bird may hang on the wind or sometimes hover. Nests on cliffs or in trees. The 2–4 eggs hatch at 2-day intervals after 35 days. Young fly after 50 days, but are dependent on parents for a further 40–55 days.

adult

dark adult
(from below)

BIRDS OF PREY

50–60 cm

| J | F | M | A | M | J |
| J | A | S | O | N | D |

Rough-legged Buzzard
Buteo lagopus

ID FACT FILE

Size: Slightly larger than Buzzard

All birds: Very variable. Usually pale with paler underparts

Bill: Small, dark with yellow base and hooked

In flight: Often hovers, long wings held in shallow 'V', dark belly patch, dark tail-band and dark wing-tips

Voice: Louder and lower than Buzzard

Lookalikes: Buzzard (p.69), Honey Buzzard (p.67), Osprey (p.64)

A pale buzzard of the Arctic tundra or Scandinavian uplands which winters in central and eastern Europe. It feeds on small mammals, especially voles and lemmings, and in years when prey is plentiful it may extend its breeding range southwards. It frequently hovers when hunting. It nests on the ground, on rocky ledges or in trees. The 3-4 eggs hatch at 2 day intervals after 28 days. The young fly after 40 days and are dependent on parents for a further 20-35 days.

adult

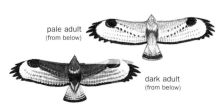

pale adult
(from below)

dark adult
(from below)

BIRDS OF PREY

48–56 cm

| J | F | M | A | M | J |
| J | A | S | O | N | D |

Marsh Harrier
Circus aeruginosus

ID FACT FILE

SIZE: Buzzard-sized

MALE: Dark body, grey head, grey wings and tail

FEMALE: Dark. Crown and front of wings straw-coloured

JUVENILE: Like an all-brown female

BILL: Hooked

IN FLIGHT: Long tail, long wings often held in shallow 'V'

VOICE: Usually silent

LOOKALIKES: Buzzard (p.69), Hen Harrier (p.72), Montagu's Harrier (p.73)

The drainage of many European wetlands has reduced the population of this large bird of prey. It still breeds in some of the larger marshes and in river valleys where it hunts small mammals and birds. Northern populations migrate south in autumn and some reach Africa. The nest is a pile of reeds and sticks on marshy ground, and 3–8 eggs are laid 2–3 days apart. Young hatch after 35 days and fly 35 days later.

adult male

adult female

adult male
(from above)

adult female
(from above)

BIRDS OF PREY

44–52 cm

J	F	M	A	M	J
J	A	S	O	N	D

Hen Harrier
Circus cyaneus

ID FACT FILE

Size: Smaller than Buzzard

Male: Blue-grey with black wing-tips and white rump

Female: Larger than male, brown with white rump

Juvenile: Similar to female with more orange underparts

Bill: Hooked

In flight: Rather narrow wings, forms shallow 'V' when soaring

Voice: Usually silent

Lookalikes: Buzzard (p.69), Marsh Harrier (p.71), Montagu's Harrier (p.73)

A bird of open, upland country, usually away from human disturbance. Northern populations move south or west to lowland or coastal areas for the winter and may roost communally. Often flies low, quartering the ground as it searches for small mammals and birds. Nests on the ground, laying 4–6 eggs which hatch after 30 days. Incubation starts from the first egg so ages of young are staggered. Young fly after 35 days.

adult female

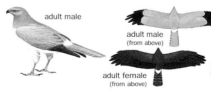

adult male

adult male
(from above)

adult female
(from above)

43–47 cm

J	F	M	A	M	J
J	A	S	O	N	D

Montagu's Harrier
Circus pygargus

ID FACT FILE

SIZE: Smaller than Buzzard

MALE: Grey with black wing-tips. One black bar on upper wings and 2 below; some streaks on belly and flanks

FEMALE: Brown with small white rump

JUVENILE: Like female, with more orange underparts

BILL: Hooked

IN FLIGHT: Long narrow wings

VOICE: Usually silent

LOOKALIKES: Hen Harrier (p.72), Marsh Harrier (p.71), Buzzard (p.69)

In most parts of Europe populations of Montagu's Harriers have declined this century. They breed in dry fields and meadows and feed on small mammals and birds. In autumn they migrate to Africa. The nest is on the ground on a mound of grasses or reeds among tall vegetation. The 4–5 eggs hatch after 28 days. Young fly after 35 days and are dependent on their parents for a further 10 days or so.

adult female

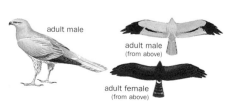

adult male

adult male
(from above)

adult female
(from above)

BIRDS OF PREY

48–62 cm

| J | F | M | A | M | J |
| J | A | S | O | N | D |

Goshawk
Accipiter gentilis

A resident in forests throughout mainland
Europe, and recently has recolonised some
forests in the British Isles. A secretive hunter
which catches birds and mammals after a
short, fast chase. The nest of sticks is built in a
large tree. The 3–4 eggs hatch after 35 days,
and the young are fed and tended by the
female. Young males fly after 35 days, young
females, being larger, fly a few days later.

ID FACT FILE

SIZE: Larger than
Sparrowhawk;
female almost
Buzzard-sized

ADULT: Dark
brown above,
white and finely
barred below.
Broad bands on
tail, dark head,
white stripe over
eye

FEMALE: Larger
than male

BILL: Hooked

IN FLIGHT: Like
large sparrow-
hawk, with
shorter wings
and longer tail
than Buzzard

VOICE: Usually
silent

LOOKALIKES:
Sparrowhawk
(p.75), Buzzard
(p.69), Hen
Harrier (p.72)

adult female

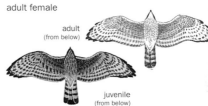

adult
(from below)

juvenile
(from below)

BIRDS OF PREY

28–38 cm

J	F	M	A	M	J
J	A	S	O	N	D

ID FACT FILE

SIZE: Kestrel-sized

MALE: Blue-grey back, barred rufous under-parts

FEMALE: Much larger, with brown back

BILL: Hooked

IN FLIGHT: Broad, rounded wings, long tail. Rapid wing-beats followed by glide

VOICE: Shrill *kee, kee, kee* at nest, but usually silent

LOOKALIKES: Goshawk (p.74), Kestrel (p.76)

Sparrowhawk
Accipiter nisus

This small woodland hawk feeds on small birds which it pursues in flight. It never hovers like a kestrel and will hunt along woodland edges, hedges and even in gardens. Females, being larger, catch prey up to the size of pigeons. Sparrowhawks nest in trees and lay 5 eggs. Young hatch after 33 days and fly after 24–30 days, but are dependent on parents for a further 20–30 days.

adult female

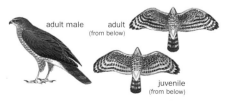

adult male

adult
(from below)

juvenile
(from below)

32–35 cm

| J | F | M | A | M | J |
| J | A | S | O | N | D |

ID FACT FILE

Size: Medium-sized bird of prey

Male: Chestnut back with black spots. Blue-grey head and tail

Female: Streaky brown

Juvenile: Similar to female

Bill: Hooked, grey with yellow base

In flight: Long, pointed wings. Frequently hovers

Voice: Loud *kee-kee-kee*

Lookalikes: Merlin (p.77), Hobby (p.78), Sparrowhawk (p.75)

Kestrel
Falco tinnunculus

At home in many habitats, from remote mountains to town centres. Frequently hunts beside busy roads. Found throughout Europe, but migratory in the north and east. Feeds on small mammals, birds and insects which it hunts by hovering or from a nearby perch. Nests in holes in trees, cliffs or buildings. The 3–6 eggs hatch after 27 days. Young fly after 30 days and are fed by parents for a further month.

adult male

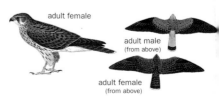

adult female

adult male
(from above)

adult female
(from above)

BIRDS OF PREY

25–30 cm

| J | F | M | A | M | J |
| J | A | S | O | N | D |

ID FACT FILE

Size: Smaller than Kestrel

Male: Bluish back, reddish streaked breast, black band at end of tail

Female: Larger than male. Brown back, barred tail

Juvenile: Like female

Bill: Hooked

In flight: Often close to the ground, with short powerful wing strokes followed by a glide

Voice: Shrill, rapid *ki-ki-ki*

Lookalikes: Kestrel (p.76), Sparrowhawk (p.75)

Merlin
Falco columbarius

This small falcon of wild, open countryside in N Europe migrates south in Europe for the winter and may visit estuaries and farmland. Chases small birds in flight. Usually nests on the ground among heather, but may use an old crow's nest in a tree, laying 3–5 eggs which hatch after 28 days. Young fly after about 25 days and are dependent on their parents for a further 2–4 weeks.

adult male

adult female

adult male
(from above)

adult female
(from above)

30–36 cm

BIRDS OF PREY

J	F	M	A	M	J
J	A	S	O	N	D

Hobby
Falco subbuteo

ID FACT FILE

Size: Kestrel-sized

Adult: Dark blue-grey above, dark 'moustache' heavily streaked below, reddish flanks

Juvenile: Like adult but browner

Bill: Hooked

In flight: Long pointed wings give appearance of large Swift. Fast, stream-lined, agile

Voice: Scolding *kew kew kew*

Lookalikes: Kestrel (p.76), Merlin (p.77), Peregrine (p.79)

This is a summer migrant to fields and open woodland of lowland Europe, where it feeds on large insects and birds, both of which it catches in flight. It is so agile that it often takes Swallows and martins and sometimes Swifts. It nests in trees, in the old nests of other species. The 3 eggs, laid in June, hatch after 28 days. Young fly after 28 days, but are dependent on parents for a further month.

adult male

adult female   adult (from above)

36–48 cm

| J | F | M | A | M | J |
| J | A | S | O | N | D |

Peregrine
Falco peregrinus

ID FACT FILE

Size: Woodpigeon-sized

Adult: Blue-black back, buff underparts with black barring, black head and 'moustache', white cheeks and chin

Juvenile: Brown upperparts, streaked underparts

Bill: Hooked

In flight: Pigeon-like but with long glides.

Voice: Chattering *kek, kek, kek*

Lookalikes: Hobby (p.78)

A large, fast falcon of open country with cliffs and crags for nest sites. Visits lowlands and coastal marshes in winter. A migrant in N Europe, a resident in the south. The Peregrine catches birds after a dramatic 'stoop', or captures them by surprise in fast, level flight. Hunts from a great height, dropping on to prey at about 160 kph. It lays 3 or 4 eggs which hatch after 29 days. Young fly after 35 days but are dependent on their parents for a further 2 months.

adult summer

juvenile   adult (from above)

37–42 cm

| J | F | M | A | M | J |
| J | A | S | O | N | D |

Red Grouse/Willow Grouse

Lagopus lagopus

ID FACT FILE

SIZE: Larger than Partridge

RED GROUSE (BRITISH ISLES–A): Male dark reddish-brown, with red wattle over eye. Female browner

WILLOW GROUSE (EUROPE–B): Head, neck and back brown, rest of body white. In winter the bird is all white

BILL: Small, dark, hooked

IN FLIGHT: Rapid whirring wings followed by glide with wings bowed

VOICE: Scolding *go back-back-back*

LOOKALIKES: Ptarmigan (p.81), Grey Partridge (p.87), Black Grouse (p.82)

These grouse live on tundra, moors, and bogs of N Europe, feeding on vegetation, especially heather, willow and birch. They usually feed on the ground, but also in trees. The nest is on the ground. The 6–9 eggs hatch after 22 days. The young leave the nest and mostly feed themselves. They can fly at 12 days, but are not fully grown until 30 days and not fully independent for a further month.

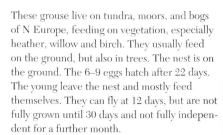

adult Red Grouse

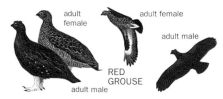

adult female

adult female

adult male

adult male

RED GROUSE

adult male

34–36 cm

| J | F | M | A | M | J |
| J | A | S | O | N | D |

Ptarmigan
Lagopus mutus

ID FACT FILE

Size: Larger than Grey Partridge

Male in summer: Dark brown, greyer in autumn

Male in winter: White with black tail

Female in summer: Camouflaged brown

Female in winter: Similar to male

Bill: Black, hooked at tip

In flight: Rapid flaps followed by glide. White wings, even in summer

Voice: Croaks and rasping noises

Lookalikes: Red Grouse (p.80)

This bird of the Arctic tundra also lives on the tundra-like tops of mountains further south in Europe. It is a resident, but may be forced to move short distances by severe weather conditions. It feeds on plant material. The nest is a shallow scrape, and 5–8 eggs hatch after 21 days. Young leave the nest and feed themselves soon after hatching. They fly after about 10 days, but are not fully independent until 10 weeks.

adult male summer

adult autumn

adult female summer

adult female winter

adult male winter

adult male summer

40–55 cm

| J | F | M | A | M | J |
| J | A | S | O | N | D |

Black Grouse
Tetrao tetrix

ID FACT FILE

SIZE: Larger than Red Grouse

MALE: Black with white wing-bars, and white under a lyre-shaped tail

FEMALE: Grey-brown, forked tail, slight wing-bars

BILL: Small, hooked

IN FLIGHT: Whirring wings followed by glides, sometimes quite high

VOICE: Hissing and cooing when displaying

LOOKALIKES: Red Grouse (p.80), Capercaillie (p.83)

The mock battles of male 'Blackcock' at dawn on their 'leks' is one of the dramas of open northern or upland forests. This grouse feeds on buds, berries and some insects, usually found on the ground, but sometimes in trees. A resident, it usually nests on the ground and lays 6–11 eggs which hatch after 25 days. Young quickly leave the nest and feed themselves. They fly after 10 days, but stay with parents for about 3 months.

Blackcock displaying

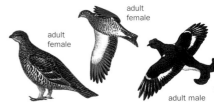

adult female

adult female

adult male

60–67 cm

J	F	M	A	M	J
J	A	S	O	N	D

Capercaillie
Tetrao urogallus

ID FACT FILE

Size: Largest grouse

Male: Dark brown and black, with white shoulder. Long tail is fanned out in display

Female: Smaller, brown with dark bars; reddish patch on breast

Bill: Small, pale, horn-coloured

In flight: Longish, broad tail and broad wings

Voice: Series of rattling sounds ending in loud *pop* during display

Lookalikes: Black Grouse (p.82)

The giant turkey-like grouse of northern and upland forests is secretive and difficult to observe. Males display together and attract females to traditional 'leks' in spring. Feeds mainly on the ground on buds and shoots, but also in the tops of trees. Nests on the ground. Lays 7–11 eggs which hatch after 24 days. Young quickly leave the nest and feed themselves. They fly by 3 weeks, and are fully grown by 3 months.

adult male displaying

adult male

adult female

adult female

53–89 cm
(including tail)

J	F	M	A	M	J
J	A	S	O	N	D

Pheasant
Phasianus colchicus

ID FACT FILE

SIZE: Larger than any partridge

MALE: long tail, colourful, red face, green head and neck, bronze body. Some have white ring round neck

FEMALE: Sandy-brown with darker marks

BILL: Small, pale

IN FLIGHT: Rounded wings, long pointed tail. Flies with whirring wings and a glide

VOICE: Crowing *krook-kock*

LOOKALIKES: None in area

This attractive bird has been introduced to many parts of Europe from Asia for hunting. It lives in countryside with woods and farms, and eats a wide range of food including grain, worms, spiders and green shoots. A resident, it nests on the ground among thick vegetation, laying 6–15 eggs which hatch after 23 days. Young leave the nest and feed themselves; they fly at 12 days and remain with female until about 2 months.

male breeding plumage

adult male

adult female   juvenile

adult female

16–18 cm

| J | F | M | A | M | J |
| J | A | S | O | N | D |

Quail
Coturnix coturnix

ID FACT FILE

SIZE: Smallest European game bird

MALE: Sandy-brown with darker marks. Variable head-pattern of pale and dark stripes

FEMALE: Similar, but head-pattern less distinctive

BILL: Small, curved

IN FLIGHT: Shallow but fast wing-beats

VOICE: *Whip, whip-whip*, most obvious at dawn or dusk

LOOKALIKES: Grey Partridge (p.87)

A small, secretive game bird which arrives from Africa in varying numbers each spring. It breeds in open countryside away from trees and hedges, feeding on seeds and insects. Its call may be heard at dawn and dusk, but the bird is hard to see. The nest is in a shallow scrape, and the 8–13 eggs hatch after 17 days. Young feed themselves and are cared for by the female. They can flutter off the ground at 11 days and fly at 18 days. They stay in a family party for 30–50 days.

adult male

adult female

adult male

GAME BIRDS AND RAILS

32–34 cm

| J | F | M | A | M | J |
| J | A | S | O | N | D |

Red-legged Partridge
Alectoris rufa

ID FACT FILE

Size: Larger than Grey Partridge

Adults: Plain sandy-brown, striped sides. Black and white face-pattern, red legs

Juvenile: Less distinctive markings

Bill: Red and curved

In flight: Rapidly whirring wings, but often runs rather than flies

Voice: Rhythmic chuffing

Lookalikes: Grey Partridge (p.87), Quail (p.85)

This partridge lives in open, often dry habitats and arable farmland. It is resident in SW Europe, but also successfully introduced to Britain. Feeds on seeds, leaves and insects. Makes several nests and female uses one. The 10–16 eggs hatch after 23 days. May have two broods, one cared for by each parent. Young mainly feed themselves and fly after 10 days. They are fully grown at 50 days and join family parties for their first winter.

adult

adults

GAME BIRDS AND RAILS

29–31 cm

J	F	M	A	M	J
J	A	S	O	N	D

Grey Partridge
Perdix perdix

ID FACT FILE

Size: Smaller than Pheasant

Male: Plump, brown and grey, with a reddish face. Dark crescent on breast

Female: Like male but with crescent reduced or absent

Bill: Pale blue-green, curved

In flight: Rapid wing-beats followed by glide on down-curved wings

Voice: Grating *kirr-ick*

Lookalikes: Red-legged Partridge (p.86), Pheasant (p.84), Quail (p.85)

Open country and arable farms with hedges or other shrubs and bare areas of dry soil for dust-bathing are home for this resident game bird. Changing farming practices have caused a decline in many places. It feeds on plant material and insects, nesting on the ground in dense vegetation. The 10–20 eggs hatch after 23 days and young mainly feed themselves. They can fly by 15 days, reach their parents' weight by 100 days and stay as a family for their first winter.

adult

adults

23–28 cm

J	F	M	A	M	J
J	A	S	O	N	D

Water Rail
Rallus aquaticus

ID FACT FILE

Size: Smaller than Moorhen

Adults: Brown with dark streaks. Blue-grey underparts, white streaks on flanks, white under tail

Bill: Long, slightly curved, red

Juvenile: Like adult but less well marked

In flight: Weak with trailing legs

Voice: Repetitive *kek* and pig-like squeals

Lookalikes: Moorhen (p.90), Corncrake (p.89)

The secretive and slim-bodied Water Rail walks or swims through the densely vegetated wet places where it lives. Cold winter weather sometimes forces it into more open places. It is migratory in the east, resident in the south and west, and feeds on plants and small creatures including fish. The nest is among thick vegetation on the ground. The 6–11 eggs hatch after 19 days. Young fly after 20 days. There are often 2 broods.

adult

adult

27–30 cm

J	F	M	A	M	J
J	A	S	O	N	D

Corncrake
Crex crex

ID FACT FILE

Size: Smaller than Moorhen

All Birds: Yellowish-buff with darker marks on back

Bill: Stubby, yellow-brown

In flight: Chestnut on wings. Legs dangle

Voice: Repetitive, grating *creck-creck*, mostly at dusk or after dark

Lookalikes: Water Rail (p.88), Grey Partridge (p.87), Quail (p.85)

The Corncrake is gradually disappearing from much of Europe. Arriving from Africa in spring, it skulks in dense grasslands, pastures and hayfields where it is more likely to be heard than seen. Changes in the way hay meadows are cut has partly caused its decline. Feeds on insects and other small animals, nests on the ground in a shallow cup of dead leaves and lays 8–12 eggs. Young hatch after 16 days, feed themselves after 3 days and fly about 34 days later.

adult

adult

32–35 cm

GAME BIRDS AND RAILS

| J | F | M | A | M | J |
| J | A | S | O | N | D |

Moorhen
Gallinula chloropus

ID FACT FILE

Size: Smaller than Coot

Adult: Blackish, with white under tail, white stripes on flanks, long greenish-yellow legs and long unwebbed toes

Bill: Red with yellow tip

Juvenile: Brown with pale throat and chin

In flight: Flutters with feet dangling, but flies much more strongly when airborne

Voice: Loud *prruck*

Lookalikes: Coot (p.91), Water Rail (p.88)

Seldom seen far from water, Moorhens can be very secretive, but frequently they are tamer in town parks. They always seem nervous, with a stealthy walk, jerky swimming and a flickering tail. They eat a wide range of vegetable and animal food. The nest is built in or over water, and the 5–9 eggs hatch after 21 days. Young are fed by parents or by young from earlier broods. They fly after 40 days. There may be 2 or 3 broods.

adult

juvenile

adult

36–38 cm

| J | F | M | A | M | J |
| J | A | S | O | N | D |

ID FACT FILE

Size: Larger than Moorhen

Adults: Silky-black, with grey-green legs. Long toes partially webbed

Bill: White, with white 'shield' above bill

Juvenile: Grey with pale face and neck

In flight: Runs across water to get airborne, and often flies with trailing legs

Voice: Far-carrying *kwock*

Lookalikes: Moorhen (p.90)

Coot
Fulica atra

Quarrelsome birds of open water, Coots flock in winter when migrants from N and E Europe join residents in the south and west. They dive to feed on vegetation and small animals, but also graze on land. They are active and noisy by night as well as by day. A bulky nest is built in shallow water among vegetation. The 6–10 eggs hatch after 21 days. Young are fed by both parents for 30 days and fly at 55 days. There may be 1 or 2 broods.

adult

juvenile

adult

40–45 cm

| J | F | M | A | M | J |
| J | A | S | O | N | D |

Oystercatcher
Haematopus ostralegus

ID FACT FILE

SIZE: Larger than Lapwing

ALL BIRDS: Black and white, with long red legs

WINTER: As summer but with white neck collar

BILL: Long, orange-red

IN FLIGHT: White wing-bar on black wings

VOICE: Piping *klep-klep*

LOOKALIKES: Avocet (p.93), Lapwing (p.100)

This distinctive wader of the seashore nests inland in some places. It feeds mostly on shell-fish, especially cockles, which it extracts from the mud with its bill and prises or jabs open. It also feeds on worms. Migratory. Large flocks form in winter in W Europe. Oystercatchers nest on the ground in the open. The 3 eggs hatch after 24 days. Young are active soon after hatching, but are fed by their parents. They fly after 28 days.

adult summer

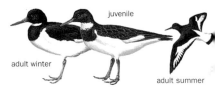

juvenile

adult winter

adult summer

42–45 cm

J	F	M	A	M	J
J	A	S	O	N	D

ID FACT FILE

Size: Similar to Oystercatcher

Adult: Black and white with long blue-grey legs and webbed feet

Juvenile: Dark brown rather than black on back

Bill: Upswept, black

In flight: Black and white with trailing legs

Voice: Liquid *kluit-kluit*

Lookalikes: Oystercatcher (p.92), Shelduck (p.42)

Avocet
Recurvirostra avosetta

Elegant, black and white wader of pools and marshes near the coast. In winter, northern birds move to sheltered estuaries in W Europe while others migrate to N Africa. The Avocet feeds on invertebrates in shallow water which it catches by sweeping its bill from side to side. It nests in the open near water and lays 2–4 eggs which take 23 days to hatch. The young feed themselves and fly after 35 days.

adult

adult

40–44 cm

J	F	M	A	M	J
J	A	S	O	N	D

Stone Curlew
Burhinus oedicnemus

ID FACT FILE

SIZE: Larger than Lapwing

ALL BIRDS: Sandy-brown with darker streaks. Rounded head, large yellow eye and long, thick legs

BILL: Short, yellow at base

IN FLIGHT: Dark wings with bold white wing-bar

VOICE: Curlew-like *coo-wee*, often heard after dark

LOOKALIKES: Golden Plover (p.98)

A rather ungainly wader, often standing hunched up and camouflaged in stony fields and other flat, open areas. A summer migrant from Africa, with a few wintering in W Europe The Stone Curlew feeds at dusk, dawn and after dark on insects and their larvae. It nests on the ground in the open, laying 2 eggs which hatch after 24 days. Young are looked after and fed by their parents for at least 36 days.

adults at nest

adult

18–20 cm

| J | F | M | A | M | J |
| J | A | S | O | N | D |

Ringed Plover
Charadrius hiaticula

ID FACT FILE

Size: Smaller than Redshank

Adult: Brown and white, with black and white head-pattern, black breast-band, orange legs

Juvenile: Scaly back, incomplete breast-band

Bill: Yellow and black

In flight: Bold white wing-bar

Voice: Piping, *tooli*

Lookalikes: Little Ringed Plover (p.96), Dotterel (p.97)

The Ringed Plover feeds like other plovers – a short run followed by a quick forward tilt of the body to pick up insects or other small creatures on or near the surface. It breeds mainly near the coast, but inland in some places, and is a summer visitor to N Europe, resident in the west, and a winter visitor further south. Ground-nesting, usually among stones. Lays 3 or 4 eggs which hatch after 23 days. Young feed themselves and fly after 24 days. There are two or three broods.

adult summer

juvenile

adult summer

14–15 cm

J	F	M	A	M	J
J	A	S	O	N	D

Little Ringed Plover
Charadrius dubius

ID FACT FILE

SIZE: Smaller than Ringed Plover

ADULT: Brown and white, with black and white face, white line above black forehead, yellow eye-ring, yellowish legs

JUVENILE: Scaly back, incomplete breast-band

BILL: Small and dark

IN FLIGHT: No wing-bar

VOICE: Flute, *peeoo*

LOOKALIKES: Ringed Plover (p.95)

Similar in its feeding action to other plovers, this is a summer migrant to areas of sand, shingle and other bare ground, usually away from the coast but generally near water. It winters in central Africa. Feeds on insects and other small creatures. The female lays 4 eggs in one of several scrapes made by the male; they hatch after 24 days. Young feed themselves and fly after 25 days. One brood usual in Scandinavia, 2 further south.

adult

juvenile

adult

20–25 cm

J	F	M	A	M	J
J	A	S	O	N	D

ID FACT FILE

Size: Smaller than Lapwing

Summer: Chestnut belly. White stripes over eyes meet at back of head. Pale breast-band

Female: Brighter than male

Autumn: Browner and less well marked

Bill: Short, black

In flight: Rapid, with no wing-bar

Voice: Soft piping *peep* call

Lookalikes: Golden Plover (p.98)

Dotterel
Charadrius morinellus

A plover of mountain tops and the far north, beyond the tree-line. The Dotterel winters in N Africa, returning as soon as its breeding grounds are free of ice. On the way it will sometimes stop over at traditional feeding grounds. It feeds on flies, beetles and other insects, and often nests on bare ground. The 3 eggs are incubated by the duller-coloured male who also looks after the young, which feed themselves and fly after 25 days.

adult summer

female spring

26–29 cm

J	F	M	A	M	J
J	A	S	O	N	D

Golden Plover
Pluvialis apricaria

A plover which breeds on bleak uplands and northern tundra. In winter it moves to lowland farmland in S and W Europe where hundreds, sometimes thousands, flock together. It feeds on beetles, worms and plant material. It nests on the ground, laying 4 eggs which hatch after 26 days. Young are cared for by both parents, and feed themselves. They fly after 25 days and are soon independent.

ID FACT FILE

SIZE: Smaller than Lapwing

SUMMER: Brown back flecked yellow, black breast and neck, variable amount of black on face

WINTER: Lacks black underparts, less yellow on back

BILL: Small, black

IN FLIGHT: White underwing, dark upper wing, slight wing-bar

VOICE: Lonely-sounding *too-ee*

LOOKALIKES: Grey Plover (p.99), Dotterel (p.97)

adult breeding plumage

adult winter

adult winter

adult winter

WADERS

27–30 cm

| J | F | M | A | M | J |
| J | A | S | O | N | D |

Grey Plover
Pluvialis squatarola

ID FACT FILE

SIZE: A little larger than Golden Plover

SUMMER: Black belly, foreneck and face; grey spangled back

WINTER: Grey spotted upperparts, pale grey underparts

BILL: Short, black

IN FLIGHT: White rump, white wing-bar, blackish 'armpit'

VOICE: Mournful, far-carrying, *pee-oo-wee*

LOOKALIKES: Golden Plover (p.98)

This beautiful black, white and grey wader breeds in the high Arctic and winters on muddy seashores and estuaries. In summer it feeds on insects, in winter on worms, molluscs and crustaceans. Usually solitary when feeding, but many gather in large flocks when feeding grounds are covered at high tide. Some non-breeding birds spend the summer well south of their breeding range.

adult breeding plumage

adult winter

adult winter

adult winter

WADERS

Lapwing
Vanellus vanellus

ID FACT FILE

SIZE: Smaller than Woodpigeon

ALL BIRDS: Dark metallic green and white, orange under tail, thin crest, long legs

JUVENILE: Shorter crest, buff tips to feathers on back

BILL: Black, stubby

IN FLIGHT: Broad, rounded black and white wings. Rather floppy flight

VOICE: Wheezy, drawn-out *pee-wit*

LOOKALIKES: None

Lapwings breed in open, flat country including farmland and coastal marshes. The aerial display is exciting and noisy as a Lapwing rises and tumbles over its territory. After nesting flocks form and travel to find suitable feeding areas free of frost. There is true migration, but severe weather triggers additional movements. Nests on the ground. The 4 eggs hatch after 26 days. Young feed themselves, fly at about 35 days and leave their parents soon after.

adult spring

juvenile

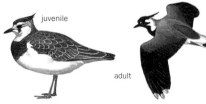

adult

WADERS

23–25 cm

J	F	M	A	M	J
J	A	S	O	N	D

Knot
Calidris canutus

ID FACT FILE

Size: Smaller than Redshank

All birds: Plump with short neck and medium-long black legs

Summer: Brick-red underparts, spangled grey back

Winter: Greyer back, grey underparts

Bill: Medium length, black

In flight: Faint pale wing-bar

Voice: Low *knut*

Lookalikes: Dunlin (p.106), Sanderling (p.102), Purple Sandpiper (p.104)

An arctic breeding species which migrates long distances. Those that flock to W European estuaries are either migrants from Siberia en route to Africa or winter visitors from Greenland and Canada. These vast winter flocks feed on invertebrates found in the mud between the high and low tide lines. At high tide they roost in tight flocks on the upper shore or on nearby fields. In Europe they are rarely seen away from the coast.

adult winter

adult summer

adult winter

WADERS

20–21 cm

| J | F | M | A | M | J |
| J | A | S | O | N | D |

Sanderling
Calidris alba

ID FACT FILE

SIZE: Larger than Ringed Plover

SUMMER: Reddish-brown back, head and breast; white underparts

WINTER: Pale grey back, white underparts. Often has blackish mark on front of wings. Black legs

BILL: Black, medium length

IN FLIGHT: Dark wings, broad white wing-bar

VOICE: Quiet *kip*

LOOKALIKES: Dunlin (p.106), Knot (p.101), Little Stint (p.103)

In Europe the Sanderling visits sandy beaches, running like a clockwork toy along the edge of the sea, or probing the sand around pools left by a retreating tide. It feeds on small invertebrates and often snatches food as it is washed ashore. It breeds in the high Arctic where females will sometimes lay 2 clutches of eggs, one of which is incubated by the male. Those that visit Europe are migrants from either Greenland or Siberia.

adult winter

adult summer

adult winter

WADERS

12–14 cm

ID FACT FILE

Size: Smaller than Dunlin

Summer: Reddish-brown with paler underparts

Winter: Scaly grey back, pale breast

Juvenile: Brown scaly back with pale 'V' pattern

Bill: Short, black, delicate

In flight: White wing-bar, white sides to rump and tail

Voice: Short sharp *tit*

Lookalikes: Dunlin (p.106), Common Sandpiper (p.120)

Little Stint
Calidris minuta

The Arctic tundra is the breeding ground for this delicate wader. Its migration takes it to central and southern Africa, and migratory Little Stints pass through Europe on a broad front, with a tendency for there to be more juveniles further west. It feeds with a rapid action on invertebrates, especially fly and beetle larvae. It is most likely to be seen around the muddy edges of inland pools or brackish pools near the coast.

juvenile

adult summer

adult winter

20–22 cm

J	F	M	A	M	J
J	A	S	O	N	D

Purple Sandpiper
Calidris maritima

ID FACT FILE

Size: Smaller than Turnstone

Summer: Scaly grey and chestnut back, dark head, heavily streaked breast and streaks on flanks

Winter: Slate-grey with paler belly

Bill: Long, dark with yellow base

Legs: Rather short and yellow

In flight: White sides to rump, faint wing-bar

Voice: Generally silent, *weet-wit* flight call, swallow-like twittering

Lookalikes: Turnstone (p.121)

For most of the year this dumpy wader is to be found on rocky coasts or is attracted to man-made features such as breakwaters. It feeds on invertebrates which it picks up from the water's edge or from newly exposed seaweed. Nests on open ground in the Arctic or the Scandinavian uplands. Lays 4 eggs which it incubates for 21 days. Young feed themselves and are cared for by the male.

adult winter

adult summer

adult winter

18–19 cm

J	F	M	A	M	J
J	A	S	O	N	D

ID FACT FILE

Size: Similar to large Dunlin

All birds: White rump, longer legs and longer neck than Dunlin

Summer: Brick-red, mottled back

Autumn: Dunlin-like grey and white; pale stripe over eye

Juvenile: Like autumn adult with scaly back

Bill: Long, down-curved

In flight: White wing-bar, white rump

Voice: Twittering *chirrup*

Lookalikes: Dunlin (p.106), Knot (p.101)

Curlew Sandpiper
Calidris ferruginea

This long-distance migrant breeds in Siberia. Some winter in central and southern Africa while others fly to SE Asia or Australia. Those that migrate through Europe sometimes stop and feed on muddy or sandy coasts, saltmarshes or margins of inland lakes. They probe in the soft mud for invertebrates. Before migration their weight increases from 50 g to 83 g, enabling them to fly 3,000 km before stopping to feed.

adult winter

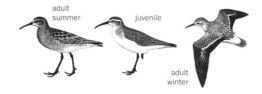

adult summer

juvenile

adult winter

WADERS

16–20 cm

| J | F | M | A | M | J |
| J | A | S | O | N | D |

Dunlin
Calidris alpina

ID FACT FILE

Size: Smaller than Redshank

All birds: Rather hunched

Summer: Rufous spotted back, grey head and neck, black belly

Winter: Grey-brown head and upperparts, pale underparts

Juvenile: Browner, scaly back and streaked breast

Bill: Black, variable length, often down-curved at tip

In flight: White wing-bar, white sides to rump

Voice: In flight a rough *treep*

Lookalikes: Little Stint (p.103), Knot (p.101), Common Sandpiper (p.120)

Dunlins vary in size. The bill and leg length of northern breeding birds is noticeably shorter than that of southerly breeders. Outside the breeding season Dunlins gather in large flocks on seashores and estuaries rich in invertebrates, but also visit fringes of inland lakes. The Dunlin breeds on upland moors and on coastal grassland in the north, laying 4 eggs in a nest on the ground. The young hatch after 21 days and fly when about 20 days old.

adult winter

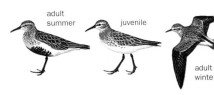

adult summer

juvenile

adult winter

20–30 cm

ID FACT FILE

Size: Male similar to Redshank, female smaller

All birds: Long legs, small head, humped back

Male (breeding): Loose ruff

Male (non-breeding): Scaly grey-brown back, buff head and breast, white underparts

Female: Like small non-breeding male

Bill: Shortish and drooping

In flight: Long-winged, loose action. White ovals on tail

Voice: Generally silent

Lookalikes: Redshank (p.116), Greenshank (p.117)

Ruff
Philomachus pugnax

The extraordinary neck-ruffs are a variety of colours and used as they dance and posture at their 'leks'. Females mate with the most successful (often black-feathered) males. Ruffs are summer visitors to inland marshes, steppe and wet meadows. Most winter in Africa, while a few remain in Europe. They feed mostly on insects and their larvae. Females incubate the eggs and look after the young; 4 eggs hatch after 20 days and the young fly 25 days later.

adult male winter

adult male summer variants

adult winter

WADERS

17–19 cm

J	F	M	A	M	J
J	A	S	O	N	D

ID FACT FILE

SIZE: Smaller than Snipe

ALL BIRDS: Large head, dark brown with darker and paler markings, especially 2 yellowish stripes on back and crown

BILL: Long (but not as long as Snipe), straight, pale with darker tip

IN FLIGHT: Weak-looking; more direct than Snipe

VOICE: Usually silent

LOOKALIKES: Snipe (p.109)

Jack Snipe
Lymnocryptes minimus

A small snipe with secretive habits, the Jack Snipe is reluctant to fly if disturbed, preferring to rely on camouflage for protection. If it does take to the wing it does so quietly and usually settles again quickly. When walking it shuffles and bounces. Breeds in north-eastern marshlands and winters in W Europe and in Africa. Feeds on insects, worms and seeds. The nest is on the ground among short vegetation; 4 eggs hatch after 24 days.

adult

adults

WADERS

25–27 cm

J	F	M	A	M	J
J	A	S	O	N	D

Snipe
Gallinago gallinago

ID FACT FILE

SIZE: Slightly smaller than Redshank

ALL BIRDS: Short legs. Brown with darker marks and buff streaks; buff stripe through centre of crown

BILL: Very long, straight

IN FLIGHT: Zigzag flight when alarmed

VOICE: Harsh *scapp* in flight, *chippa-chippa* song in spring

LOOKALIKES: Jack Snipe (p.108), Woodcock (p.110)

Snipe use their long sensitive bills to probe for worms and other invertebrates hidden in soft mud. They display over their marshland breeding territories, using their tail-feathers to produce a bleating sound called 'drumming'. Migrants leave N Europe in autumn and many winter in wet fields and marshes in the west and south. They nest on the ground and lay 4 eggs which hatch after 18 days. Young fly 19 days later.

adult

adults

WADERS

33–35 cm

J	F	M	A	M	J
J	A	S	O	N	D

Woodcock
Scolopax rusticola

ID FACT FILE

Size: Larger than Snipe

All birds: Plump, dark reddish-brown with delicate darker barring, black bars across crown

Bill: Very long, straight

In flight: Display (called 'roding') is just above tree-tops, bill pointing down, owl- or bat-like, flight path often repeated

Voice: Roding call is a series of low growls followed by sharp *twisick*

Lookalikes: Snipe (p.109)

A secretive bird of woodlands with damp areas where it can probe for earthworms and other invertebrates. In spring males look for mates by flying slowly and low calling as they fly. Woodcocks from N Europe migrate south and west in autumn. The bird nests on the ground among low vegetation, laying 4 eggs which hatch after 22 days. Young may be able to fly from the 10th day but remain with the parent for 5–6 weeks.

adult

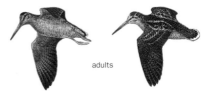

adults

40–44 cm

J	F	M	A	M	J
J	A	S	O	N	D

ID FACT FILE

SIZE: Similar to Oystercatcher

MALE (SUMMER): Brick-red, mottled back, barred breast, white belly

FEMALE (SUMMER): Less colourful than male

WINTER: Grey upperparts, paler underparts, pale stripe over eye

JUVENILE: Similar to winter adult, but more buff, scaly back

BILL: Very long, and straight

IN FLIGHT: Black tail, white rump, white wing-bars

VOICE: Urgent *weeka-weeka*

LOOKALIKES: Bar-tailed Godwit (p.112), Spotted Redshank (p.115)

Black-tailed Godwit
Limosa limosa

This large, elegant wader breeds on wet meadows, wet heaths or moorland. At other times it moves to sheltered coasts and estuaries. It feeds on insects and their larvae, worms, and seeds and other plant material. European birds migrate to S and W Europe or Africa for the winter. The nest is on the ground among short vegetation and there are 3 or 4 eggs. Young hatch after 22 days and feed themselves, but are cared for by both parents.

adult winter

adult summer

adult winter

37–39 cm

J	F	M	A	M	J
J	A	S	O	N	D

Bar-tailed Godwit

Limosa lapponica

ID FACT FILE

SIZE: Smaller than Black-tailed Godwit

MALE (SPRING): Head, neck and underparts rich rufous; grey-brown scaly back

FEMALE (SPRING): A little more rufous than in winter

WINTER: Streaky grey-brown upper-parts, paler and less streaky below

BILL: Very long, slightly up-curved

IN FLIGHT: No wing-bar. White back and rump

VOICE: Low *kirruc* call in flight

LOOKALIKES: Black-tailed Godwit (p.111), Whimbrel (p.113)

A large wader of the high Arctic which visits coasts in SW Europe and Africa after breeding. It probes with its long bill in its search for food. In its hunt for insects, molluscs, crustaceans and marine worms it often visits sandy shores, whereas the Black-tailed Godwit is more likely to be seen on muddy estuaries or pools near the sea. Some food-rich areas attract large numbers of birds which are spaced out while feeding but flock together at high tide.

adult winter

adult summer

adult winter

WADERS

40–42 cm

J	F	M	A	M	J
J	A	S	O	N	D

ID FACT FILE

SIZE: Smaller than Curlew

ALL BIRDS: Brown, stripy, with pale stripe through centre of crown and pale stripe above eye

BILL: Down-curved, shorter than Curlew

IN FLIGHT: Pale 'V'-shaped rump

VOICE: Series of about 7 short sharp whistles

LOOKALIKES: Curlew (p.114), Bar-tailed Godwit (p.112)

Whimbrel
Numenius phaeopus

This small curlew is a long-haul migrant, breeding in the far north and migrating as far as southern Africa. Some visit coasts on migration, others fly on a broad front across Europe. Whimbrels breed in open country, often in upland peat bogs or on tundra. They feed on insects, berries and marine creatures including crabs. They nest among short vegetation, laying 3–4 eggs which hatch after 27 days. Young feed themselves and fly after 35 days.

adult

adults

WADERS

50–60 cm

J	F	M	A	M	J
J	A	S	O	N	D

Curlew
Numenius arquata

The bubbling song is given over upland meadows and moorlands where breeding takes place. The 'curlew' call may also be heard outside the breeding season on mudflats and sandbanks where Curlews feed on worms, crabs and other crustaceans by probing at low tide. The nest is on the ground among short vegetation; 4 eggs are incubated for 27 days. Young feed themselves and are cared for by both parents until they fly at about 32 days.

ID FACT FILE

SIZE: The largest European wader

ALL BIRDS: Grey-brown with darker streaks and other marks, no pronounced head-pattern

MALE: Bill shorter than female

BILL: Very long, down-curved

IN FLIGHT: Pale 'V'-shaped rump

VOICE: Bubbling *cor-wee*

LOOKALIKES: Whimbrel (p.113)

adult

adults

29–31 cm

| J | F | M | A | M | J |
| J | A | S | O | N | D |

Spotted Redshank
Tringa erythropus

ID FACT FILE

Size: Larger than Redshank

Breeding: Velvety-black, spotted back

Winter: Grey with white underparts, scaly back, pale stripe over eye

Juvenile: Grey spotted back, barred under-parts

Bill: Long, reddish at base

Legs: Long and reddish

In flight: White underwings, darker above with oval white patch on back

Voice: Flight call *chew-it*

Lookalikes: Redshank (p.116), Black-tailed Godwit (p.111)

This is a particularly handsome wader in breeding plumage. It nests in the far north and visits southerly coasts and some inland pools either as a passage migrant or a winter visitor. It wades, often in deep water, chases prey or swims and up-ends like a duck. It hunts small marine creatures, insects and fish. Breeding takes place in wet, often wooded areas, where the male does much of the incubation and cares for the young.

adult winter

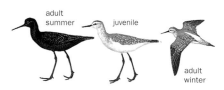

adult summer   juvenile

adult winter

WADERS

27–29 cm

| J | F | M | A | M | J |
| J | A | S | O | N | D |

Redshank
Tringa totanus

ID FACT FILE

SIZE: Smaller than Lapwing

SUMMER: Olive-brown, heavily streaked head and breast, streaked white underparts

WINTER: More uniform appearance

BILL: Slender, medium length, red base

LEGS: Long, red

IN FLIGHT: White trailing edges to wings, white rump

VOICE: Ringing *tew*, repeated *teup*

LOOKALIKES: Spotted Redshank (p.115), Greenshank (p.117), Ruff (p.107)

A noisy and often obvious wader which nests in wet meadows, pastures and marshes, including saltmarshes. The Redshank is usually found near the sea in winter. Its food includes shrimps, snails and worms, and it has an even-paced, jerky walk as it hunts its prey. The nest is among grasses and the 4 eggs hatch after 24 days. Young are cared for by both parents (especially the male), feed themselves and fly at 25–35 days.

adult winter

adult summer

WADERS

30–33 cm

J	F	M	A	M	J
J	A	S	O	N	D

ID FACT FILE

Size: Larger than Redshank

All birds: Upright stance, greenish-grey back. White breast and underparts are spotted in summer

Bill: Long, slightly upswept

Legs: Long, greenish

In flight: Dark wings, white 'V' on back

Voice: Ringing *tew-tew-tew*

Lookalikes: Redshank (p.116), Spotted Redshank (p.115), Ruff (p.107)

Greenshank
Tringa nebularia

A tall, elegant wader of northern bogs, often with a scattering of trees nearby. Summer migrant to N Europe, Greenshanks also visit lakes and estuaries as passage migrants usually seen singly or in very small groups. A few remain in Europe all winter, but most fly to Africa. Feeds on insects, crustaceans and fish. Nests on the ground; 4 eggs hatch after 24 days. Young feed themselves, are cared for by both parents and fly after 25 days.

adult winter

adult summer

21–24 cm

| J | F | M | A | M | J |
| J | A | S | O | N | D |

Green Sandpiper
Tringa ochropus

ID FACT FILE

Size: Smaller than Redshank

Summer: Dark speckled back, white underparts

Winter: Less speckling on back

Bill: Medium length, dark

Legs: Greenish-grey

In flight: All-dark wings, white rump

Voice: Flight call *weet-a-weet-weet*

Lookalikes: Wood Sandpiper (p.119), Common Sandpiper (p.120)

This wader nests off the ground, usually in old nests of other birds, in wet woodlands near flowing water. Feeds on insects and other invertebrates. Breeds in NE Europe and migrates to Africa, but some winter around freshwater margins in S and W Europe and others occur as migrants. The 4 eggs hatch after 20 days. Young feed themselves, are cared for by both parents and fledge after 28 days, although the female may leave a little before that.

adult winter

adult summer

19–21 cm

J	F	M	A	M	J
J	A	S	O	N	D

Wood Sandpiper
Tringa glareola

ID FACT FILE

SIZE: Smaller than Redshank

ALL BIRDS: Brown spotted back, pale underparts, white stripe over eye

BILL: Medium dark

LEGS: Yellowish

IN FLIGHT: Feet project beyond tail. Pale underwing, white rump but less contrasted than Green Sandpiper

VOICE: *Chiff-if-if*, given in flight

LOOKALIKES: Green Sandpiper (p.118), Common Sandpiper (p.120)

This northern breeding wader visits S Europe as a passage migrant en route to central and southern Africa. Those seen in late summer are feeding mainly on insects to increase their body weight by 20–30 per cent in readiness for their non-stop flight across both the Mediterranean and the Sahara Desert. The bird nests on the ground, laying 4 eggs which hatch after 22 days. Young are cared for mainly by the male and fly after 30 days.

adult winter

juvenile

19–21 cm

J	F	M	A	M	J
J	A	S	O	N	D

Common Sandpiper
Actitis hypoleucos

ID FACT FILE

SIZE: Smaller than Redshank

ALL BIRDS: Bobbing walk. Brown above, white below, with white shoulder patch and brown smudge on sides of breast

BILL: Medium, horn-coloured

LEGS: Rather short, grey or yellowish

IN FLIGHT: Wings 'flicker' below level of body, often appearing bowed. White wing-bars, white sides to tail

VOICE: Shrill *tee-we-we*

LOOKALIKES: Dunlin (p.106), Green Sandpiper (p.118), Wood Sandpiper (p.119)

A summer visitor to many parts of Europe where there is fresh water, especially fast-flowing rivers and streams, either at sea level or high in hills, also visits lake edges on migration. Winters in Africa. Feeds mainly on insects, and nests on the ground, usually among vegetation. Lays 4 eggs which hatch after 21 days and are cared for by both parents. Young have weak flight after 15 days and full flight at about 26 days.

adult

adult summer

WADERS

22–24 cm

J	F	M	A	M	J
J	A	S	O	N	D

Turnstone
Arenaria interpres

ID FACT FILE

Size: Larger than Ringed Plover

Summer: Chestnut and black back, black and white head and breast, white belly

Winter: Blackish head and back, white underparts

Bill: Shortish, stout, black

Legs: Reddish

In flight: Striking white marks on wings, back, rump and tail

Voice: Twittering *kitititit*

Lookalikes: Oystercatcher (p.92), Ringed Plover (p.95), Redshank (p.116)

Picking, probing and snapping at insects as it pushes over stones or moves seaweed with its bill is the Turnstone's characteristic feeding action. It breeds mainly around the Arctic coasts and migrates to other rocky coasts, as far south as S Africa. Ground-nesting, laying 4 eggs which hatch after 22 days. Young feed themselves. Both parents care for them at first, but female may leave before they fly at 20 days.

adult winter

adult male summer

adult female summer

adult winter

18–19 cm

J	F	M	A	M	J
J	A	S	O	N	D

Red-necked Phalarope
Phalaropus lobatus

ID FACT FILE

SIZE: Size of Ringed Plover

FEMALE (SUMMER): Grey head, white chin, chestnut neck, darker back with gold marks

MALE (SUMMER): Less boldly marked than female

WINTER: Grey and white with dark eye-patch and dark crown

JUVENILE: Brownish back with buff stripes; buff breast

BILL: Long, fine and black

IN FLIGHT: Fast, twisting. White wing-bar, white sides to tail

VOICE: Low *twick*

LOOKALIKES: Dunlin (p.106)

Feeds while swimming and spinning to stir up invertebrates. It also wades and picks food from the surface of the water. Its summer home is around small pools in the far north. Many winter in the Arabian Sea, often far from land. On migration it visits both coasts and inland lakes. Nests on the ground. The 4 eggs are incubated by the male which is less colourful than the female. Young hatch after 17 days and are cared for by the male.

adult female summer

juvenile

adult winter

adult winter

46–51 cm

J	F	M	A	M	J
J	A	S	O	N	D

Pomarine Skua
Stercorarius pomarinus

ID FACT FILE

Size: Smaller than Herring Gull

Adult: Elongated, spoon-shaped central tail feathers

Light phase: Dark above, with pale underparts and a dark cap

Dark phase: Dark above and below

Juvenile: Usually dark and heavily barred, but some paler. Lacks long central tail feathers

Bill: Dark, heavy-looking

In flight: Deep-chested, heavy body, white wing panel, light or dark underparts

Voice: Usually silent

Lookalikes: Arctic Skua (p.124), Great Skua (p.125)

When these heavy-looking skuas are seen migrating along the coasts of Europe they are moving between their breeding grounds in the Arctic tundra and their wintering grounds in the open Atlantic Ocean, north of the equator. Their migration routes may take them over land in some places. In summer they feed on lemmings, the eggs and young of other birds, and fish. Like other skuas, they will often chase seabirds to make them disgorge their catch.

adult summer

pale adult summer

dark adult summer

41–46 cm

| J | F | M | A | M | J |
| J | A | S | O | N | D |

Arctic Skua
Stercorarius parasiticus

ID FACT FILE

SIZE: Smaller than Herring Gull

ADULT: 2 long central tail feathers

LIGHT PHASE: Dark above, dark cap

DARK PHASE: Dark above and below

JUVENILE: Varies from dark to pale. Heavily barred, especially on underparts. Lacks long central tail feathers

BILL: Blue-grey, powerful-looking

IN FLIGHT: Powerful and acrobatic, with bursts of speed. White wing-panel on underwing

VOICE: Mewing and barking when nesting

LOOKALIKES: Other skuas (pp.123–5)

This aerial pirate breeds on moorland or tundra around the coasts of N Europe. It often chases other seabirds and forces them to disgorge their catch. When nesting it attacks possible predators, including humans. It winters at sea, off the coasts of Africa and S America. Ground nesting, sometimes in colonies. The 2 eggs are incubated for 25 days. Young fly after 30 days and stay with their parents for 3–5 weeks.

adult

pale adult summer

dark adult summer

53–58 cm

| J | F | M | A | M | J |
| J | A | S | O | N | D |

Great Skua
Stercorarius skua

ID FACT FILE

Size: As Herring Gull

All birds: Dark brown and streaked, barrel-like body

Juvenile: Like adult but with more rufous, spotted rather than streaked plumage

Bill: Large and strong

In flight: Like a large, heavy, short-tailed gull. Rapid accelera-tion, white wing-flashes

Voice: Harsh scolding calls when breeding

Lookalikes. Young Herring Gull (p.132), Pomarine Skua (p.123), Arctic Skua (p.124)

A powerful seabird which feeds mainly on fish that it catches itself, scavenges or obtains by piracy. It also kills other seabirds. Recently it has spread from Iceland and the Faeroes to N Scotland and Scandinavia. It winters at sea, and nests in colonies on grassy cliff-tops or moorland. The 2 eggs hatch after 29 days. Young are fed by both adults, and fly at 44 days.

adult

adult

39 cm

J	F	M	A	M	J
J	A	S	O	N	D

Mediterranean Gull

Larus melanocephalus

ID FACT FILE

Size: As Black-headed Gull

All birds: Bulky, thick neck

Summer: Black head, white around eye

Winter: White head, dark smudge round and behind eye

First winter: Pale grey. Head like winter adult, dark outer primaries, black stripe at rear of wing and tip of tail

Bill: Heavy-looking, red

Legs: Red

In flight: Pale back, white wing-tips, drooping bill

Voice: Tern-like *kee-ah*

Lookalikes: Black-headed Gull (p.128)

This attractive gull has spread beyond the Mediterranean and visits other S European coasts, especially outside the breeding season. Numbers nesting in Russia have also increased and many migrate to the Mediterranean for the winter. It feeds on insects in summer and fish and other marine creatures at other times. It nests in colonies in fields and marshes near water, laying 3 eggs which hatch after 35 days. The young fly 35 days later.

adult summer

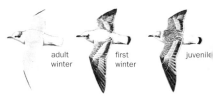

adult winter

first winter

juvenile

25–27 cm

| J | F | M | A | M | J |
| J | A | S | O | N | D |

Little Gull
Larus minutus

ID FACT FILE

Size: Smaller than Black-headed Gull

Summer: Black head, grey back, no black wing-tips

Winter: Head white with dark crown and spot behind eye

Juvenile: Strongly marked with 'W' pattern on wings

First winter: Like winter adult but dark 'W' pattern

Bill: Small and dark

In flight: Buoyant, tern-like. Dark underwing, pale rear edge to wing

Voice: Usually silent

Lookalikes: Black-headed Gull (p.128), Black Tern (p.139)

The smallest European gull nests in freshwater marshes in NE Europe. It migrates over land, but winters mainly in coastal areas and may be seen singly or in small flocks. It feeds on insects in summer and fish and small marine creatures at other times. Rather tern-like as it dips to take food from the surface of the water. Nests in colonies on the ground and lays 2 or 3 eggs which hatch after 23 days. Young fly after 21 days.

adult spring

adult winter

first winter

juvenile

34–37 cm

J F M A M J
J A S O N D

ID FACT FILE

Size: Smaller than Herring Gull

Summer: Dark brown head, pearl-grey back, black wing-tips

Winter: White head, dark mark behind eye

Juvenile: Ginger-brown marks on head and back

First winter: Dark bars on wings, black band on tail

Bill: Deep red

Legs: Deep red, feet webbed

In flight: White stripe on front edge of wings

Voice: Scolding *karrr*

Lookalikes: Little Gull, (p.127), Mediterranean Gull (p.126), Common Tern (p.136)

Black-headed Gull
Larus ridibundus

A familiar gull over much of Europe. It breeds inland or on coastal marshes and visits farmland town parks and sheltered coasts mostly in autumn and winter when resident birds in W Europe are joined by migrants from the N and E. These gulls eat insects and worms, but also visit rubbish tips. Nests on the ground, usually in colonies. The 2 or 3 eggs hatch after 23 days. Both parents care for the young, which leave the nest after 10 days and fly 15 days later.

adult summer

adult winter / first winter / juvenile

40–42 cm

Common Gull
Larus canus

ID FACT FILE

SIZE: Smaller than Herring Gull

ADULT: White head, grey back, dark eyes. Elegant

WINTER: Heavily streaked head

FIRST WINTER: Strongly marked head, grey back, brown 'juvenile' wings

BILL: Small, yellow, no red spot

LEGS: Yellowish-green with webbed feet

IN FLIGHT: Grey back, white spots on black wing-tips

VOICE: Mewing *kee-aah*

LOOKALIKES: Herring Gull (p.132), Kittiwake (p.130)

This gentle-looking gull breeds in N Europe on rocky islands, shingle bars, marshes and upland moors. It feeds on aquatic insects, worms and fish. Common Gulls migrate southwards to grasslands, agricultural land and some sea coasts. Many roost on inland reservoirs. They nest in colonies, mainly on the ground, and lay 3 eggs. Young hatch after 23 days and are cared for by both parents. They leave the nest after 5 days and fly about 30 days later.

adult summer

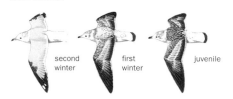

second winter   first winter   juvenile

38–40 cm

| J | F | M | A | M | J |
| J | A | S | O | N | D |

Kittiwake
Rissa tridactyla

ID FACT FILE

SIZE: Smaller than Common Gull

ADULT: White with blue-grey back, black wing-tips and rounded head

JUVENILE: Smudge behind eye, black collar, black 'W' pattern in flight, black-tipped forked tail

BILL: Fine, yellow, no red spot

LEGS: Black with webbed feet

IN FLIGHT: Long grey wings with triangular black tips

VOICE: Drawn-out *kitti-wake* heard at colonies

LOOKALIKES: Common Gull (p.129), Little Gull (p.127)

A true 'sea gull', nesting in large noisy colonies on precipitous sea cliffs in NW Europe and spending the rest of the year at sea. Many young spend their first 2 years off the coast of Greenland. Nests are cemented to cliff ledges with seaweed and droppings. Recently buildings near the sea have been colonised. The 2 eggs hatch after 27 days. Young are cared for by both parents and fly after about 40 days.

adult summer

adult summer

adult winter

juvenile

52–67 cm

| J | F | M | A | M | J |
| J | A | S | O | N | D |

Lesser Black-backed Gull
Larus fuscus

ID FACT FILE

Size: Similar to Herring Gull but slimmer

Adult: Elegant, white with dark grey back

Scandinavian race: Black back

Juvenile: Dark brown with almost uniformly dark back

Bill: Yellow with red spot

Legs: Yellow with webbed feet

In flight: Rather long narrow wings. More graceful and buoyant than Herring Gull

Voice: Gruff laughing calls

Lookalikes: Great Black-backed Gull (p.133), Herring Gull (p.132)

Closely related to the Herring Gull, Lesser Black-backs are summer migrants to many of their northerly breeding colonies, although recently those in Britain have increasingly overwintered. Nests on islands, dunes or moors and increasingly winters in coastal areas. Eats a wide range of food, including scavenging at rubbish tips and predating other birds. The nest built of seaweed or grasses, is on the ground, and the 3 eggs hatch after 24 days. Young fly at 30–40 days.

adult summer

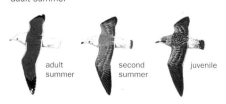

adult summer

second summer

juvenile

55–67 cm

| J | F | M | A | M | J |
| J | A | S | O | N | D |

Herring Gull
Larus argentatus

ID FACT FILE

Size: Larger than Black-headed Gull

Adult: Pearl-grey back, fierce eye with yellow iris

Winter: Heavy streaking on back of head

Juvenile: Mottled brown, bill becoming paler and back greyer with age

Bill: Powerful, with hooked tip. Yellow with red spot

Legs: Flesh-pink with webbed feet

In flight: Broad wings, heavy-looking

Voice: Wailing, laughing, crying

Lookalikes: Common Gull (p.129), Lesser Black-backed Gull (p.131)

A familiar gull around the coasts of NW Europe. It is seldom seen far out to sea and also visits inland rubbish tips, farmland and parks. It roosts on the sea along sheltered coasts and on reservoirs. Herring Gulls eat a variety of food including carrion and offal from fishing boats. They nest on open, often sloping ground and sometimes on buildings. The 3 eggs hatch after 28 days. Young leave the nest after 3 days and fly at about 35 days.

adult summer

adult summer

second summer

first winter

64–78 cm

| J | F | M | A | M | J |
| J | A | S | O | N | D |

Great Black-backed Gull
Larus marinus

ID FACT FILE

Size: Large, bulky gull

Adult: Angular head, thick neck, black back with small amount of white on wing-tips

Juvenile: Dark brown chequered upperparts, paler head and tail

Bill: Long, deep and powerful. Yellow with red spot

Legs: Pink legs with webbed feet

In flight: Heavy looking. Broad wings with large white spots at tips

Voice: Short gruff barks

Lookalikes: Lesser Black-backed Gull (p.131)

The largest of the gulls eats a variety of food and also uses piracy to capture food. It frequently kills other birds, especially young seabirds. It breeds on small islands, cliff-tops and sometimes marshes or moorland. Migratory in the north, resident further south, but generally seen near the coast. The nest is a mound of vegetation. The gull lays 2 or 3 eggs which hatch after 27 days. Young are cared for by both parents and fly after about 7–8 weeks.

adults summer

adult summer

second summer

first winter

36–41 cm

| J | F | M | A | M | J |
| J | A | S | O | N | D |

Sandwich Tern
Sterna sandvicensis

ID FACT FILE

SIZE: Larger than Black-headed Gull

ADULT (SPRING): White, very pale grey back, black cap, untidy crest

ADULT (SUMMER): Forehead whitens, back becomes paler

WINTER: White forehead, spotted crown, untidy crest

BILL: Long, black with yellow tip

IN FLIGHT: Long wings, long bill, short tail streamers. Rather stiff flight

VOICE: Rasping *kirrit*

LOOKALIKES: Common Tern (p.136), Arctic Tern (p.137), Little Tern (p.138)

This large, pale tern nests in noisy colonies on mainly sandy seashores. It plunge-dives to catch surface-living fish such as sand-eels. Some birds migrate as far as southern Africa while others winter around S European coasts. Lays 1 or 2 eggs in a shallow scrape. Young hatch after 21 days and may join a large crèche. They fly after 28 days, but may depend on their parents for the first 4 months.

adult summer

adult

juvenile

33–38 cm

| J | F | M | A | M | J |
| J | A | S | O | N | D |

Roseate Tern
Sterna dougallii

ID FACT FILE

Size: Similar to Black-headed Gull

Adult (summer): Very pale back, long tail streamers project beyond wings when perched, rosy flush to breast in spring, black cap

Juvenile: Rather like small Sandwich Tern

Bill: Long, black with red base

Legs: Red, relatively long

In flight: Slender, narrow wings, long tail streamers

Voice: Shrill *chew-ick*

Lookalikes: Common Tern (p.136), Arctic Tern (p.137), Sandwich Tern (p.134)

An increasingly rare breeding species on sand-dunes, sand spits or coastal islands in W Europe and the Azores. It winters along the coast of W Africa. It catches small fish by plunge-diving from the air. The nest is on the ground, often sheltered by a rock or vegetation. Lays 1 or 2 eggs which hatch after 23 days. Young fly at 22–30 days and are dependent on their parents for several weeks.

adult summer

adult summer

juvenile

31–35 cm

J	F	M	A	M	J
J	A	S	O	N	D

Common Tern
Sterna hirundo

An elegant summer visitor to beaches, fresh-water marshes and flooded sand and gravel quarries. Winters along the African coast. Catches small fish by plunge-diving. Adults display over their breeding territories. Nests on the ground usually, in colonies, and lays 1–3 eggs which hatch after 21 days. The young leave the nest after a few days and are fed by both parents. They fly after 25 days, but may be dependent on their parents for 2–3 months.

ID FACT FILE

Size: Smaller than Black-headed Gull

Summer: Pale grey back, large flat head, black cap

Winter: White forehead

Juvenile: Browner back, shorter wings and tail

Bill: Red with black tip

Legs: Short, red

In flight: Long pointed wings, long tail streamers, dark wedge mark on outer primaries and translucent inner primaries

Voice: Rasping *kee-aaarr*

Lookalikes: Black-headed Gull (p.128), other terns (pp.134–9)

adult summer

adult summer

juvenile

33–35 cm

J	F	M	A	M	J
J	A	S	O	N	D

Arctic Tern
Sterna paradisaea

ID FACT FILE

Size: Smaller than Black-headed Gull

Summer: Grey back, black cap, white cheeks. Smaller and more rounded head than Common Tern. Some white on forehead in late summer

Juvenile: Grey and white, scaly back, white fore-head, clean-looking

Bill: Long, red

Legs: Short, red

In flight: Light and buoyant. Wings long and tapering, long forked tail, paler wing-tips than Common Tern

Voice: Higher than Common Tern

Lookalikes: Other terns (pp.134–9)

No bird sees more daylight than the Arctic Tern. Many breed in the arctic and winter near Antarctica. They nest in colonies on beaches and islands usually close to the sea, sometimes with Common Terns. The Arctic Tern catches fish by plunge-diving. It lays 1–3 eggs in a shallow scrape on the ground. Young hatch after 20 days and soon shelter in surrounding vegetation. They fly after 21 days but are dependent on their parents for several weeks.

adult summer

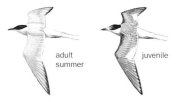

adult summer

juvenile

22–24 cm

| J | F | M | A | M | J |
| J | A | S | O | N | D |

Little Tern
Sterna albifrons

ID FACT FILE

Size: Smaller than Common Tern

Adult: Grey back, black cap, white forehead, black stripe through eye, yellow legs

Juvenile: Scaly back, brown cap

Bill: Long, yellow with black tip

In flight: Often hovers. Dumpy with large head and long slim wings, dark outer flight feathers, forked tail

Voice: Excited *kik-kik*

Lookalikes: Common Tern (p.136)

The smallest tern is a summer visitor to shingle or sandy beaches. In some parts of Europe it follows major rivers to breed inland on shingle islands or other bare areas. Winters along the coast of W Africa. Frequently hovers before diving to catch fish. Nests in colonies or alone often very close to the water's edge. The 1–3 eggs hatch after 20 days and young shelter near the nest. They fly after 19 days and are fed by their parents for several weeks.

adult summer

adult summer

juvenile

22–24 cm

ID FACT FILE

Size: Smaller than Black-headed Gull

Summer: Sooty-black body, slate-grey wings, white under tail

Autumn: White body, black crown extending behind eye, dark shoulder mark, paler wings

Bill: Long, black

In flight: Leisurely, often swooping down to the water or hovering

Voice: Harsh *kreert*

Lookalikes: Common Tern (p.136), Little Gull (p.127)

Black Tern
Chlidonias niger

A summer visitor to freshwater marshes where it mainly feeds on insects and their larvae. Its flight is erratic and it frequently dips to pick food delicately from the surface of the water. The birds winter mainly in the coastal region of tropical W Africa and visit larger lakes and reservoirs on migration. Lays 2–4 eggs on a mat of floating vegetation. Young hatch after 21 days, fly between 15 and 25 days and are independent soon after.

adult summer

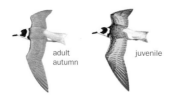

adult autumn

juvenile

38–41 cm

| J | F | M | A | M | J |
| J | A | S | O | N | D |

ID FACT FILE

Size: Largest member of the auk family

Summer: Dark brown or black back and head, white underparts. Some birds have white 'spectacle' mark round eye

Winter: Neck and lower face becoming white

Bill: Dagger-like, dark brown

In flight: Whirring wings, legs protruding beyond tail

Voice: Growling *aaarrr*

Lookalikes: Razorbill (p.141), Black Guillemot (p.142), Puffin (p.144)

Guillemot
Uria aalge

Large colonies of this penguin-like seabird breed on the dramatic sea-cliffs of NW Europe. After breeding it spends the rest of the year at sea. When feeding it chases fish underwater. The single, pear-shaped egg is laid on a cliff ledge or flat rock and hatches after 30 days. Young leave the cliff at 20 days, several weeks before being able to fly. They are fed by their parents at sea.

adult summer

adult winter

AUKS

37–39 cm

J	F	M	A	M	J
J	A	S	O	N	D

Razorbill
Alca torda

ID FACT FILE

SIZE: Slightly smaller than Guillemot

SUMMER: Head, back and upperparts mostly black, underparts white

WINTER: White neck, chin and cheeks

BILL: Black with white marks, deep and laterally flattened

IN FLIGHT: Fast on small, narrow, whirring wings

VOICE: Growling call when breeding

LOOKALIKES: Guillemot (p.140), Puffin (p.144), Black Guillemot (p.142)

Breeds on sea-cliffs, but in more sheltered positions than Guillemot, such as between boulders and in crevices. Its colonies in NW Europe are occupied only for the breeding season, the rest of the year being spent at sea. Feeds on fish which it chases underwater. The single egg hatches after 36 days. Young fly from the cliffs at about 18 days and are then cared for by parents at sea.

adult summer

adult winter

AUKS

30–32 cm

J	F	M	A	M	J
J	A	S	O	N	D

Black Guillemot
Cepphus grylle

ID FACT FILE

SIZE: Smaller than Guillemot

SUMMER: Black with white patches on wings. Red legs and feet

WINTER: White with mottled back

BILL: Black, red inside

IN FLIGHT: All black in summer, with white wing-patches

VOICE: Thin peeps and whistles when nesting

LOOKALIKES: Guillemot (p.140), Razorbill (p.141)

This guillemot feeds closer to the shore and is less colonial than other members of the auk family. It remains around its rocky breeding sites during the winter, often feeding along the edge of pack ice in the Arctic. It feeds on fish which are caught by diving, and nests in crevices in sea-cliffs, among boulders and in holes in buildings. The 1 or 2 eggs hatch after 23–40 days, depending on the number of eggs, and young fly 40 days later.

adult winter

adult summer

17–19 cm

J	F	M	A	M	J
J	A	S	O	N	D

Little Auk
Alle alle

ID FACT FILE

Size: Similar to Starling

All birds: Dumpy, short-necked

Summer: Black upperparts, white underparts

Winter: Neck and lower part of face becoming white

Bill: Short, stubby, black

In flight: Fast, flickering wingbeats, and frequent changes of direction

Voice: Mainly silent away from breeding grounds

Lookalikes: Puffin (p.144), Guillemot (p.140), Razorbill (p.141)

Vast colonies of Little Auks nest on inaccessible cliffs in the high Arctic. Southern colonies are smaller. After the breeding season is over and food becomes scarce, Little Auks move south to winter in the N Atlantic, following colder currents and avoiding the warmer water of the Gulf Stream. They are unusual inland unless autumn gales blow migrating birds off course and then large numbers may be 'wrecked' along the coast or even far inland.

adult winter

adult summer

adult winter

26–29 cm

J	F	M	A	M	J
J	A	S	O	N	D

Puffin
Fratercula arctica

This attractive seabird is a summer visitor to islands and sea-cliffs in NW Europe. For the rest of the year it lives on the open sea. Fish are caught by diving and swimming under-water. Puffins nest in colonies in burrows and lay 1 egg which hatches after 39 days. Young are fed by both parents for about 40 days the leave their burrow at night and head for the open sea.

ID FACT FILE

SIZE: Smaller than town pigeon

ALL BIRDS: Large head. Upright on land, duck-like on the sea

SUMMER: Black and white; clown-like expression

WINTER: Dusky cheeks, bill less colourful

JUVENILE: Smaller than adult, cheeks very dusky, black stubby bill

BILL: Triangular, colourful

IN FLIGHT: Large head and bill, broad outer wing, rapid wing-beats

VOICE: Growling *arr ar-ar-ar*

LOOKALIKES: Other auks (pp.140–4)

adult summer

adult winter

PIGEONS

31–33 cm

J	F	M	A	M	J
J	A	S	O	N	D

Collared Dove
Streptopelia decaocto

ID FACT FILE

Size: Smaller than town pigeon

All birds: Pinkish-grey with black half-collar

Bill: Small, dark

In flight: Dark wing-tips, black and white pattern under tail, pale outer tail feathers. Parachuting display

Voice: Monotonous *co-coo-cok*

Lookalikes: Turtle Dove (p.146), Feral Rock Dove (p.147)

This species originated in India and spread dramatically northwest across Europe during the 20th century. It is mainly resident and feeds on grain, other seeds, berries and grasses. It is common in towns, villages, parks and gardens. It lays 2 eggs in a flimsy nest of twigs in a tree or bush. Young hatch after 14 days, fly at 14 days and are independent a week later. There may be 3–6 broods a year.

adult

adults

PIGEONS

26–28 cm

| J | F | M | A | M | J |
| J | A | S | O | N | D |

Turtle Dove
Streptopelia turtur

ID FACT FILE

SIZE: Slightly smaller than town pigeon

ALL BIRDS: Slim, with small blue-grey head, pinkish breast, dark neck-marks, mottled back

BILL: Small, horn-coloured

IN FLIGHT: Rapid, manoeuvrable, glides on spread wings. Black tail with white border

VOICE: Loud cat-like purring

LOOKALIKES: Collared Dove (p.145), Feral Rock Dove (p.147), Woodpigeon (p.144)

A small dove which winters in central Africa and returns in spring to S and central Europe, where its purring song is a familiar sound of summer. Feeds on the ground, eating mainly plant material, especially seeds. Nests in woodland edges, copses and tall hedges, laying 1 or 2 eggs in a flimsy nest of twigs. Young hatch after 13 days and fly about 20 days later. There are 2, or sometimes 3, broods a year.

adult

adults

PIGEONS

31–34 cm

J	F	M	A	M	J
J	A	S	O	N	D

ID FACT FILE

Size: Medium-sized pigeon

Wild Rock Dove: Blue-grey, black bars on wings, white rump

Feral Rock Dove: May be similar to wild form, but plumage varies from very dark to white, with pied and brown forms

Bill: Small, grey

In flight: Wild form shows white rump and black bars on wings

Voice: Soft cooing

Lookalikes: Stock Dove (p.148), Collared Dove (p.145), Turtle Dove (p.146), Woodpigeon (p.149)

Rock Dove
Columba livia

Rock Doves are residents of remote sea-cliffs and other rocky areas (see map below). They are the ancestors of tame and town pigeons. Feral pigeons are common throughout Europe and have a wide range of plumage colours. They nest on natural or artificial ledges or in a cavity. The 2 eggs hatch after 16 days. Young fly after 35 days and may remain with parents for 10 more days. There are often 5 broods a year.

adult

feral variants

adult

PIGEONS

32–34 cm

| J | F | M | A | M | J |
| J | A | S | O | N | D |

Stock Dove
Columba oenas

ID FACT FILE

SIZE: As town pigeon

ALL BIRDS: Blue-grey, with purple sheen on neck, pinkish breast, slate-grey wings with short black bars

BILL: Small, pale

IN FLIGHT: No white on wings but 2 short black bars. Wings held in 'V' in display

VOICE: Hollow-sounding *ooo-woo*

LOOKALIKES: Woodpigeon (p.149), Rock Dove (p.147)

Found in parkland, avenues of old trees, and copses where it nests in holes in trees or in cliff- or rock-faces. Likes water nearby, where it frequently drinks. Feeds mainly on seeds, buds and leaves. Forms flocks in winter, sometimes with Woodpigeons. A migrant in N and E Europe, resident elsewhere. Lays 2 eggs which hatch after 16 days. Young fly between 20 and 30 days. There are 2 or more broods in a year.

adult

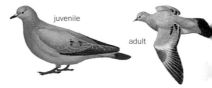

juvenile

adult

PIGEONS

40–42cm

J	F	M	A	M	J
J	A	S	O	N	D

ID FACT FILE

Size: The largest pigeon

Adult: Heavy-looking, blue-grey, with small head and pinkish breast; white marks on neck

Juvenile: Lacking white on neck

Bill: Yellow, pink base

In flight: White crescents on wings. 'Wing-claps' in display; glides on down-curved wings

Voice: Gently cooing *too-COO-woo-woo*

Lookalikes: Stock Dove (p.148), Turtle Dove (p.146)

Woodpigeon
Columba palumbus

A successful woodland species, but also familiar on farmland and, more recently, in towns and gardens. N and E European Woodpigeons are migrants and fly southwest in winter when flocks gather on agricultural land and form large roosts. Eats seeds, leaves and other plant material. Lays 1–2 eggs in a flimsy nest of twigs. Young hatch after 17 days and fly at 30 days, but may leave earlier if disturbed. There are usually 2 broods.

adult

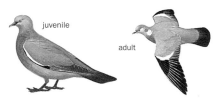

juvenile

adult

32–34 cm

J	F	M	A	M	J
J	A	S	O	N	D

Cuckoo
Cuculus canorus

ID FACT FILE

SIZE: Smaller than Kestrel

ADULT: Grey head and upperparts, barred under-parts, long tail, long wings which droop when perched

JUVENILE: Reddish-brown, barred back, white spot on nape

BILL: Small, slightly curved

IN FLIGHT: Hawk-like, fast and straight, with shallow wing-beats. Pointed wings, long tail

VOICE: Male has repetitive cuckoo song, female, bubbling call

LOOKALIKES: Kestrel (p.76), Sparrowhawk (p.75), Nightjar (p.157)

The Cuckoo's song is generally welcomed as a sign of spring. Woodland, reed-beds, moorland and farmland are some of the habitats used by Cuckoos. Dunnock, Meadow Pipit, Brambling and Redstart are all hosts for Cuckoos in Europe. Up to 25 eggs are laid by one female in different nests. The young Cuckoo hatches after 12 days, systematically ejects the other eggs and flies after 17 days, but may be dependent on its hosts for several weeks.

adult

immature

38–42 cm

| J | F | M | A | M | J |
| J | A | S | O | N | D |

Ring-necked Parakeet
Psittacula krameri

ID FACT FILE

Size: Larger than Kestrel

Male: Pale yellow-green, long tail, thin black line round neck

Female: Like male without ring round neck

Bill: Red, flattened and down-curved

In flight: Fast, flickering wing-beats

Voice: Harsh screech

Lookalikes: None in area

This is the only parrot breeding wild in Europe. Introduced from Africa and S Asia to parts of W Europe, this exotic species appears to be increasing in gardens, parks and orchards where its liking for soft fruit brings it into conflict with horticulturalists. It nests in holes in trees, sometimes in colonies, and lays 2–4 eggs which hatch after 22 days. Young leave the hole after 40 days and may stay with parents for up to 6 months.

adult

juvenile

adult female

33–35 cm

J	F	M	A	M	J
J	A	S	O	N	D

Barn Owl

Tyto alba

ID FACT FILE

Size: Smaller than Tawny Owl

Adult: Heart-shaped facial disc, honey-coloured back, white or buff underparts, long white legs

E Europe: Darker face, spotted buff underparts

Bill: Curved, almost hidden in feathers

In flight: Silent, buoyant, wavering. Often hovers

Voice: Many calls including loud snores from nesting birds and eerie shrieks

Lookalikes: Short-eared Owl (p.155)

A nocturnal predator which also hunts in daylight during severe weather or when feeding young. It lives in open country with some tree and also hunts over marshes, ditches and road side verges, feeding on small mammals, birds and insects. It nests in holes in buildings, trees or cliffs. The 4–7 eggs hatch at intervals after 30 days, so a brood contains young of various ages. They fly after 50 days.

adult

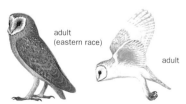

adult
(eastern race)

adult

37–39 cm

J	F	M	A	M	J
J	A	S	O	N	D

Tawny Owl
Strix aluco

ID FACT FILE

SIZE: Large, round-headed

NORMAL PLUMAGE: Camouflaged, mottled brown, with dark facial disc, dark eyes, soft streaked feathers

JUVENILE: Downy and flightless on leaving nest

BILL: Small, horn-coloured, curved

IN FLIGHT: Silent with frequent glides. Large head, broad rounded wings

VOICE: Sharp *kes-wik* and quavering *poo-hooo, poo-poo-hooo*

LOOKALIKES: Long-eared Owl (p.154), Short-eared Owl (p.155)

This plump woodland owl rarely flies in daylight and is best known for its hooting song. It feeds on small mammals and also takes birds, insects and worms. It nests in holes in trees or old nests of other large species. The 2–5 eggs hatch after 28 days. Flightless young leave the nest at about 25 days and fly a week later. They are dependent on their parents for about 3 months.

adult

adult

35–37cm

J	F	M	A	M	J
J	A	S	O	N	D

Long-eared Owl
Asio otus

ID FACT FILE

SIZE: Slightly smaller than Tawny Owl

ALL BIRDS: Cat-like face can change shape. Delicately marked brown and buff plumage, tufts on head, orange eyes

BILL: Small, partly hidden, horn-coloured

IN FLIGHT: Silent, ear-tufts hidden. Streaked under-parts, warm closely barred wings

VOICE: Low moan. Young squeak like an unoiled gate!

LOOKALIKES: Tawny Owl (p.153), Short-eared Owl (p.155)

Tall and thin when alert, this Owl becomes fluffed out when relaxed. Tufts (which are not ears!) may be raised or lowered and are hardly visible in flight. Lives in woods, but hunts mammals and birds in open country after dark In spring it has an aerial display in which it claps its wings together. Migrates, and may form communal winter roosts. Lays 3–5 eggs in an old nest of another species. Young hatch after 25 days, leave the nest at 21 days, fly at 30 days and become independent a month later.

adult

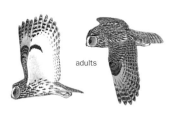

adults

37–39 cm

J	F	M	A	M	J
J	A	S	O	N	D

Short-eared Owl
Asio flammeus

ID FACT FILE

SIZE: Larger than Barn Owl

ALL BIRDS: Round face, dark 'mask', fierce yellow eyes. Straw-coloured, brown marks

BILL: Dark, partly hidden

IN FLIGHT: Long, rather narrow wings, short tail, dark mark at 'elbow' above and below, pale belly. 'Rowing', silent flight; hovers and glides

VOICE: Usually silent, but hoarse bark when alarmed. Low hooting song

LOOKALIKES: Tawny Owl (p.153), Long-eared Owl (p.154), Little Owl (p.156)

This owl hunts in daylight over open country where small mammals, especially voles, are abundant. It breeds on moors, in young forestry plantations and in marshes. Northern populations move south and west in autumn. The nest is on the ground among vegetation. The 4–8 eggs hatch after 24 days. Incubation starts with the first egg, and the young hatch over several days. They are therefore of different ages, and the oldest are more likely to survive. They fly at 35 days.

adult

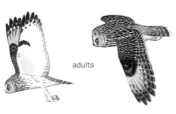

adults

21–23 cm

| J | F | M | A | M | J |
| J | A | S | O | N | D |

Little Owl
Athene noctua

ID FACT FILE

Size: Similar to Starling

All birds: Brown spotted plumage, paler streaked underparts, fierce expression, rather long legs. Bobs when curious

Bill: Hooked, yellow-green

In flight: Undulating, often close to the ground

Voice: Repetitive, yapping *kiew-kiew*

Lookalikes: Tawny Owl (p.153)

This small resident owl may be seen perched in the open during daylight. It hunts at dusk, after dark and around dawn, feeding on insects, small mammals, and worms. It lives in a variety of habitats including farmland, orchards and, in S and E Europe, it is found in hilly, arid country. It nests in holes in trees, buildings and rock faces, laying 2–5 eggs which hatch after 27 days. Young fly after 30 days and are fed by parents for a further month.

adult

adult

26–28 cm

J	F	M	A	M	J
J	A	S	O	N	D

Nightjar
Caprimulgus europaeus

The churring song of the Nightjar is a sound of summer nights in dry areas with scattered trees such as heathland, large forest clearings or young plantations. This bird is strictly nocturnal and catches flying insects, especially moths, in flight. It winters in Africa. The nest is in a scrape on the ground, and the 2 eggs hatch after 17 days. Young fly at 16 days and depend on parents for a further 16 days. There are usually 2 broods.

ID FACT FILE

SIZE: Smaller than Kestrel

ALL BIRDS: Camouflaged, delicate brown and grey marks. Perches lengthways on branch. Active at dawn and dusk

MALE: White spots on wings and tail

BILL: Small grey; large mouth

IN FLIGHT: Silent. Long pointed wings, long tail. Flies with sudden twists and turns.

VOICE: Sharp, *coo-ick* flight call. Churring song alters pitch as the bird turns its head

LOOKALIKES: Cuckoo (p.150), Kestrel (p.76); song like Grasshopper Warbler (p.196)

adult

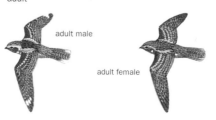

adult male

adult female

16–17 cm

J	F	M	A	M	J
J	A	S	O	N	D

ID FACT FILE

Size: Shorter body, longer wings than Swallow

Adult: Dark brown above and below; pale throat

Juvenile: Scaly back

Bill: Short, hooked, wide mouth

In flight: Fast, often in groups. Long, narrow, pointed wings, short forked tail

Voice: Harsh screams

Lookalikes: Swallow (p.169), Sand Martin (p.168)

Swift
Apus apus

Swifts spend more time in flight than most birds, catching insects, drinking and even sleeping on the wing. If they do land they have great difficulty becoming airborne again. Young leaving their nests in August may spend the next 2–3 years in the air. Swifts nest in holes in buildings or rock crevices. They lay 2 or 3 eggs which hatch after 19 days. Young fly at 42 days and migrate to Africa within a few days. The birds winter in central and southern Africa.

adult

adult

juvenile

16–17 cm

| J | F | M | A | M | J |
| J | A | S | O | N | D |

ID FACT FILE

SIZE: Slightly larger than House Sparrow

ADULT: Bright blue-green upperparts, chestnut underparts, white throat and neckpatch

JUVENILE: Duller and greener than adult

BILL: Dagger-like. Female's has red base

IN FLIGHT: Fast and direct

VOICE: Shrill whistle given in flight

LOOKALIKES: None in area

Kingfisher
Alcedo atthis

A brilliant small bird with a large head and a short tail. Found near still or slow-flowing water. Migratory in N and E Europe, mostly resident elsewhere, but some move to coasts outside the breeding season. Catches small fish by plunge-diving. The nest is in an underground chamber at the end of a tunnel which is dug by both parents. The 6 or 7 eggs hatch after 19 days and the young fly about 27 days later. There are often 2 broods.

adult female

adult female

26–28 cm

J	F	M	A	M	J
J	A	S	O	N	D

ID FACT FILE

Size: Smaller than town pigeon

All birds: Pinkish-brown. Large crest which may be raised or lowered, black and white back and tail

Bill: Long, down-curved

In flight: Bounding on broad, rounded black and white wings

Voice: Bubbling *oop-oop-oop*

Lookalikes: Jay (p.224)

Hoopoe
Upupa epops

A exotic-looking bird of S and E Europe which is sometimes seen further north. Mostly a summer visitor but resident in the extreme south. It probes the ground with its long bill as it searches for large insects. Hoopoes breed in dry places often with bare areas and buildings, trees and rocks for perches and nest sites. Nests in holes. Lays 7 or 8 eggs which hatch after 15 days. Young fly after 26 days.

adult

adult

WOODPECKERS

16–17 cm

J	F	M	A	M	J
J	A	S	O	N	D

Wryneck
Jynx torquilla

ID FACT FILE

SIZE: Slightly larger than House Sparrow

ALL BIRDS: Appear brown from a distance. Dark arrow mark on back, beautiful camouflage pattern of brown and grey

BILL: Rather short, stubby

IN FLIGHT: Hesitant and undulating

VOICE: Falcon-like *quee-quee-queel*

LOOKALIKES: None in area

Related to the woodpeckers, the Wryneck is a summer migrant to open woodlands, parks and orchards. It winters in Africa. On migration it visits a variety of habitats, from grassy cliff-tops to gardens. On the ground it hops, feeding largely on ants. Nests in holes in trees or walls, laying 7–10 eggs which hatch after 12 days. Young fly after 18 days and are dependent on parents for a further week or two.

adult

adult

31–33 cm

J	F	M	A	M	J
J	A	S	O	N	D

Green Woodpecker
Picus viridis

A large resident woodpecker which lives in woodland, small copses, farmland and parks. It often feeds on the ground, sometimes well away from trees. On the ground it moves with a series of hops. It eats ants and other insects. It excavates a nest-hole in the trunk of a tree and lays 5–7 eggs which hatch after 17 days. Young fly at 23 days and remain with parent for up to 7 weeks.

ID FACT FILE

SIZE: Similar to town pigeon

ADULT: Dark green back, yellow rump, pale underparts, red crown and nape

MALE: Red 'moustache'

JUVENILE: Similar colours but duller, spotted and barred

BILL: Long and strong

IN FLIGHT: Deeply undulating. Wings close after several strong beats

VOICE: Loud laughing-yapping call, occasional feeble drumming

LOOKALIKES: Golden Oriole (p.221)

adult female

adult

22–23 cm

J	F	M	A	M	J
J	A	S	O	N	D

ID FACT FILE

Size: Similar to Blackbird

Adult: Black and white, red under tail, white patches on back, white cheeks separated from white throat and neck by black lines

Male: Red on back of head

Juvenile: Red crown

Bill: Dark, medium-length, strong

In flight: Bounding flight. Large white wing-patches

Voice: Sharp *kik*. Drums with beak on branch in spring

Lookalikes: Lesser Spotted Woodpecker (p.164)

Great Spotted Woodpecker
Dendrocopos major

A resident of woodlands throughout Europe, this woodpecker eats insects, nuts and seeds, but also takes eggs and young birds in spring. It climbs trees in a series of hops, and is rarely seen on the ground. The nest is in a hole in a tree which the woodpecker chisels out itself. It lays 4–7 eggs which hatch after 10–13 days. Young fly after 20 days and stay with their parents for a further week.

adult female

juvenile

adult male

14–15 cm

J	F	M	A	M	J
J	A	S	O	N	D

WOODPECKERS

Lesser Spotted Woodpecker
Dendrocopos minor

A small resident species of European woodlands, except in the far north where it is partly migratory. Feeds on tree-trunks, in branches and among leaves, eating mainly insects. Rarely seen on the ground. Excavates its own nest-hole, often on the underside of a branch, and lays 4–6 eggs which hatch after 11 days. Young fly after 18 days. After nesting individuals may join with flocks of small birds which roam through woods and hedges.

ID FACT FILE

SIZE: Similar to House Sparrow

ALL BIRDS: Black and white barred back, white underparts

MALE: Red crown

FEMALE: White forehead

JUVENILE: Less clearly marked. Some red on young male's head

BILL: Short, strong

IN FLIGHT: Undulating. Barred wings

VOICE: High-pitched *pee-pee-pee*

LOOKALIKES: Great Spotted Woodpecker (p.163)

adult male

adult female

juvenile

adult male

15 cm

J	F	M	A	M	J
J	A	S	O	N	D

Woodlark
Lullula arborea

ID FACT FILE

Size: Smaller than Skylark

All birds: Like Skylark with shorter tail. Pale stripes over eyes meeting at back of head, dark mark on front edge of wing

Bill: Rather fine, horn-coloured

In flight: Short tail, dark mark on leading edge of 'blunt' wings. Weak-looking flight, circling song-flight

Voice: Sweet-sounding *kit-loo-eet*, fluty song

Lookalikes: Skylark (p.166), Tree Pipit (p.171)

Open country and woodland glades with bare ground, grass, heather or bracken and scattered trees for song-posts is the home of the Woodlark, but numbers are declining in many parts of Europe. In the north it is migratory, in the south a resident. It feeds on insects and seeds. The nest is on the ground, sheltered by vegetation. Lays 3–5 eggs which hatch after 12 days and the young fly after about 10 days. There are 2 or 3 broods.

adult

adult

18–19 cm

| J | F | M | A | M | J |
| J | A | S | O | N | D |

Skylark
Alauda arvensis

ID FACT FILE

Size: Smaller than Starling

All birds: Brown streaked back, pale underparts, streaked breast, short crest

Bill: Short, stout, horn-coloured

In flight: Broad wings with pale hind edges, white outer tail feathers. Hovers and circles while singing

Voice: Attractive long warbling song, usually given in flight

Lookalikes: Woodlark (p.165), Meadow Pipit (p.172)

The Skylark's song is typical of open countryside and farmland, as the bird hangs in the air, almost too high to see. It eats insects and seeds. Northern populations migrate; in autumn flocks fly south and west to feed on arable fields. The nest is on the ground, and the 3–5 eggs hatch after 11 days. Young leave the nest at 8 days, fly after 18 days and depend on parents for another week. There are 1–3, sometimes 4 broods in S Europe.

adult

adult

14–17 cm

J	F	M	A	M	J
J	A	S	O	N	D

Shore Lark
Eremophila alpestris

ID FACT FILE

SIZE: Smaller than Skylark

MALE (SUMMER): Yellow and black face, small black horns, sandy-grey body, less streaky than Skylark

MALE (WINTER): Indistinct face-marks

FEMALE: Less distinct face markings, more stripy back

BILL: Short, grey

IN FLIGHT: Undulating. Longish tail with dark centre and white outer feathers

VOICE: Warbling song in spring. Pipit-like *tsweet* call

LOOKALIKES: Reed Bunting (p.249)

Shore Larks breed in the far north or at high altitudes in open, often barren country. Northern birds migrate to coastal dunes, saltmarshes and beaches or to some arable areas. The bird feeds on insects and seeds and nests on the ground, often among short vegetation. It lays 2–4 eggs, which hatch after 10 days. Young may leave the nest at 9 days and fly at 16 days. There are 1 or 2 broods.

adult male summer

adult winter

12 cm

J	F	M	A	M	J
J	A	S	O	N	D

Sand Martin
Riparia riparia

ID FACT FILE

SIZE: Smaller than Swallow

ALL BIRDS: Brown above, white underparts, brown breast-band

BILL: Small, black

IN FLIGHT: Rather fluttering. Brown and white with short forked tail and pointed wings

VOICE: Twittering, chattering song

LOOKALIKES: House Martin (p.170), Swallow (p.169)

A summer visitor to much of Europe, but has declined in recent years due to drought in its wintering grounds in Africa. Returns in early spring to feed on insects which it catches in flight, often over water. Colonial; it nests in burrows which it digs for itself in river banks and other sandy cliffs. It lays 4–6 eggs which hatch after 14 days. Young fly after 22 days and depend on parents for a further week. There are 2 broods. Flocks roost in reedbeds on migration

adult

adults

17–19 cm

| J | F | M | A | M | J |
| J | A | S | O | N | D |

Swallow
Hirundo rustica

ID FACT FILE

Size: Smaller than Swift

Adults: Blue-black back, pale underparts, dull red chin, long forked tail

Juvenile: Much shorter tail

Bill: Short and broad

In flight: Dark back, pale underparts, pointed wings, forked tail

Voice: Sharp *chisick* flight call, twittering song

Lookalikes: House Martin (p.170), Sand Martin (p.168), Swift (p.158)

This summer migrant arrives each spring from Africa. Swallows are often seen perched on wires or swooping low over meadows, pastures and open water as they feed on flying insects. They avoid woodland and towns. The saucer-shaped mud nest is built under cover, in a barn or similar building. The 4 or 5 eggs hatch after 15 days. Young fly after 20 days and are dependent on their parents for a further week or more. There are 2–3 broods.

adult

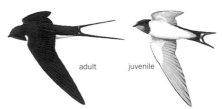

adult   juvenile

12.5 cm

J	F	M	A	M	J
J	A	S	O	N	D

House Martin
Delichon urbica

ID FACT FILE

SIZE: Smaller than Swallow

ALL BIRDS: Blue-black back, white underparts, white rump

BILL: Small, black

IN FLIGHT: Less powerful than Swallow. Broad, pointed wings, short forked tail

VOICE: *Chirrrip* call. Urgent *seep* when alarmed

LOOKALIKES: Swallow (p.169), Sand Martin (p.168)

Most House Martins have abandoned nesting on cliffs and build their cup-shaped nests of mud under the eaves of houses in towns and villages but some cliff-nesting colonies remain The House Martin winters in Africa. It eats insects which it catches in flight. Old nests are reused. The bird lays 3–5 eggs which hatch after 14 days, and the young fly between 22 an 32 days. There are 2 broods, and the young of the first brood may help feed the second.

adult summer

adults

15 cm

| F | M | A | M | J |
| A | S | O | N | D |

Tree Pipit
Anthus trivialis

ID FACT FILE

SIZE: Smaller than Skylark

ALL BIRDS: Heavier-looking and longer-tailed than Meadow Pipit. Streaked back, bold spotting on breast, fine streaks on flanks, can look pale. Wags tail

BILL: Quite heavy for a pipit

IN FLIGHT: In song-flight it spirals up and parachutes down to land on a bush or tree

VOICE: Call a hoarse *teez*. Song a series of trills ending with *seea-seea-seea*

LOOKALIKES: Meadow Pipit (p.172), Skylark (p.166), Woodlark (p.165)

Other pipits may perch on trees and bushes, but the Tree Pipit makes use of them for its attractive song-flight. It breeds on heaths, grassland or newly felled forestry areas and needs scattered trees. It winters in Africa and the largest numbers return to N and E Europe. Eats mainly insects. Nests on the ground, laying 2–6 eggs which hatch after 12 days. The young fly about 12 days later. There are 1 or 2 broods.

song flight

adult summer

14.5 cm

| J | F | M | A | M | J |
| J | A | S | O | N | D |

Meadow Pipit
Anthus pratensis

ID FACT FILE

SIZE: Similar to House Sparrow

ALL BIRDS: Brown with darker streaks on back. Streaks on breast and flanks are of uniform size and shape. Shorter tail than Tree Pipit

BILL: Thin, pointed

IN FLIGHT: Hesitant, white outer tail feathers, song given as bird rises and floats down with tail up and dangling legs

VOICE: Song a series of accelerating and decelerating notes. Flight call *seep*

LOOKALIKES: Tree Pipit (p.171), Rock Pipit (p.173), Skylark (p.166)

Meadow Pipits require no trees from which to sing. Instead they display and sing in the sky. They nest in meadowland, upland moors, lowland marshes and other open country in N Europe. In winter, northern, eastern and upland birds migrate to milder places, including farmland. Feeds on insects and plant material. Ground-nesting, laying 3–5 eggs which hatch after 13 days. Young fly at 12 days, but may leave the nest earlier. There are 2 broods.

song flight

adult

17 cm

| J | F | M | A | M | J |
| J | A | S | O | N | D |

Rock Pipit
Anthus petrosus

ID FACT FILE

Size: Larger than Meadow Pipit

Southern race: Dark, heavy streaking on breast

Northern race: Paler, plainer back with less streaking, fewer breast markings and sometimes a pinkish wash

Bill: Fine, dark

In flight: Grey outer tail feathers. Strong action, 'parachute' display

Voice: *Seeep*, less squeaky than Meadow Pipit

Lookalikes: Meadow Pipit (p.172) , Water Pipit (p.174)

Breeds around the rocky coasts of NW Europe. Northern populations migrate southwest, while others are mainly resident. Rock Pipits feed on insects, small snails and shellfish found among the rocks. They can be well-camouflaged until they fly, but their parachuting song-flight is very obvious. They nest in a hole in a cliff or bank and lay 4–6 eggs. Young hatch after 14 days and fly after 16 days. Southern birds have 2 broods.

adult

17 cm

J	F	M	A	M	J
J	A	S	O	N	D

Water Pipit
Anthus spinoletta

ID FACT FILE

SIZE: Larger than Meadow Pipit

ALL BIRDS: Pale stripe over eye, white wing-bar, longer tail than Rock Pipit, white underwing

SUMMER: Grey-brown upper-parts, pale pinkish unspotted breast

WINTER: Pale streaked breast

BILL: Shorter than Rock Pipit's

IN FLIGHT: Direct and fairly straight

VOICE: Like quiet Rock Pipit

LOOKALIKES: Rock Pipit (p.173), Meadow Pipit (p.172)

A pale pipit which breeds in the mountains of S Europe, in wet meadows, often close to the snow-line. It migrates to lower habitats in autumn and visits flooded meadows, estuaries and coastal marshes. Often seen singly, but sometimes forms flocks. Walks over water-plants like a wagtail. Eats mainly invertebrates. Nests in a bank sheltered by vegetation. The 4–6 eggs hatch after 14 days. Young fly at 14 days, and there are 2 broods.

adult

17 cm

J	F	M	A	M	J
J	A	S	O	N	D

Yellow Wagtail
Motacilla flava

ID FACT FILE

Size: Smaller than Pied Wagtail

Male: Yellow underparts, yellow, blue-grey or black head, yellow-green back. Long tail is flicked up and down

Female: Paler than male

Juvenile: Like female. Sometimes lacks yellow

Bill: Thin, pointed

In flight: Slim, long tail with white edges

Voice: Call a clear *tsweeep*

Lookalikes: Grey Wagtail (p.176), Yellowhammer (p.247)

An elegant species which looks different depending on where in Europe it breeds. It winters in Africa. Head colour ranges from yellow, through blue and grey, to black. It feeds on insects and breeds in low-lying meadows and wetland margins. Nest of grass, lined with wool or fur, is built on the ground. The bird lays 4–6 eggs which hatch after 12 days. Young fly at 16 days and stay with parents for several weeks.

adult male (yellow race) summer

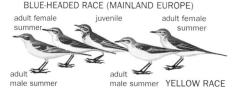

BLUE-HEADED RACE (MAINLAND EUROPE)

adult female summer

juvenile

adult female summer

adult male summer

adult male summer

YELLOW RACE (BRITISH ISLES)

18–19 cm

| J | F | M | A | M | J |
| J | A | S | O | N | D |

Grey Wagtail
Motacilla cinerea

ID FACT FILE

Size: Similar to Pied Wagtail

All birds: Slim, very long tail which is constantly flicking. Blue-grey head and back, yellow under tail

Male: Black bib, yellow breast in summer

Female: Paler underparts, white throat

Bill: Dark grey, slender

In flight: Bounding, very slim and long-tailed, with single wing-bar

Voice: Short, sharp *tizit*

Lookalikes: Yellow Wagtail (p.175)

Found near fast-flowing water, with rocks for perches, ledges for nesting and trees nearby. Often nests in uplands by mountain streams and moves to lower waters in winter. In parts of Europe this wagtail is a long-distance migrant. It feeds on insects which it picks from the ground, from the water or in flight. The nest is in a crevice, the 4–6 eggs hatch after 11 days and the young fly after 13 days. There are 2 broods.

adult male summer

juvenile

adult male winter

18 cm

J	F	M	A	M	J
J	A	S	O	N	D

ID FACT FILE

Size: Larger than House Sparrow

Adult: Black and white or grey and white. Long tail with white edges, constantly wagging up and down

Juvenile: Browner with less distinct marks, and dark patch on breast

Bill: Fine, black

In flight: Bounding, often calling

Voice: Twittering song. *Chis-ick* flight call

Lookalikes: Grey Wagtail (p.176)

Pied Wagtail
Motacilla alba

An adaptable species found near rivers, canals and lakes, also in towns, and often a surprising distance from water. Runs or flies to catch insects. Large numbers roost together in winter, sometimes in towns. Nests in a hole or crevice. The 5 or 6 eggs hatch after 12 days. Young fly after 13 days and parents feed them for a few more days. There are 2 broods. The race that breeds in the British Isles is darker than those found in most other parts of Europe.

adult male

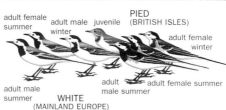

adult female summer · adult male winter · juvenile · **PIED (BRITISH ISLES)** · adult female winter

adult male summer · **WHITE (MAINLAND EUROPE)** · adult male summer · adult female summer

18 cm

J	F	M	A	M	J
J	A	S	O	N	D

Waxwing
Bombycilla garrulus

ID FACT FILE

Size: Smaller than Starling

All birds: Pinkish-brown with crest. Red wax-like tips to wing feathers

Bill: Short, strong, dark

In flight: Profile similar to slim Starling

Voice: Trilling *sirrr*

Lookalikes: None in area

A bird of northern forests which feeds on insects in summer and fruit in winter. Waxwings invade new areas if there is insufficient food. In some winters, large numbers travel across Europe in search of food and are seen in gardens and town parks where they eat berries of ornamental trees. They build a nest of twigs lined with grass and moss. The 5 or 6 eggs hatch after 14 days. Young fly after 14 days.

adult winter

18 cm

J	F	M	A	M	J
J	A	S	O	N	D

Dipper
Cinclus cinclus

ID FACT FILE

SIZE: Smaller than Starling

ALL BIRDS: Dumpy, with short cocked tail. Black and dark brown, with white breast and chin

BRITISH BIRDS: Chestnut band below white bib

JUVENILE: Grey, indistinct bib, scaly-looking

BILL: Short, dark

IN FLIGHT: Fast, direct, low, up- or downstream.

VOICE: Loud Wren-like song. Flight call is sharp *zit*

LOOKALIKES: None in area

A uniquely adapted bird which depends on fast-flowing upland rivers. It feeds on aquatic insects and their larvae, which it catches by swimming or diving. It feeds while submerged and regularly walks on river beds. Northerly populations migrate south, others are mainly resident. Builds a domed nest in a natural or man-made cavity. The 4 or 5 eggs hatch after 16 days. Young fly after 22 days. There are 1 or 2 broods.

adult

adult chestnut-bellied (Britain)

adult (continental race)

9–10 cm

| J | F | M | A | M | J |
| J | A | S | O | N | D |

Wren
Troglodytes troglodytes

ID FACT FILE

SIZE: Smaller than Blue Tit

ALL BIRDS: Tiny, dumpy; short tail often cocked above back. Brown with fine black bars, paler underparts, pale stripe over eye

BILL: Long, dark

IN FLIGHT: Fast, whirring. Broad rounded wings

VOICE: Fast, powerful warble ending with a trill. Call is a loud *tic-tic* or trill

LOOKALIKES: Dunnock (p.181), Goldcrest (p.207)

One of Europe's smallest birds, which lives in many places with low cover, from small islands to mountains. Mainly resident, but migratory in the north. Severe winters may reduce numbers, but populations can recover within a few years. It eats insects, especially beetles and spiders. The male builds several domed nests, and one is chosen and lined by the female. The 5–8 eggs hatch after 16 days and young fly after 17 days. There are 2 broods.

adult

14.5 cm

| J | F | M | A | M | J |
| J | A | S | O | N | D |

Dunnock
Prunella modularis

ID FACT FILE

SIZE: Similar to House Sparrow

ADULT: Sparrow-like body, blue-grey head and breast. Nervously flicks wings

BILL: Short, fine, blackish

IN FLIGHT: Rapid, usually low. Rounded wings

VOICE: Song Wren-like but slower and without trills. Loud piping call

LOOKALIKES: Wren (p.180), Robin (p.182), House Sparrow (p.232)

In most of Europe this is a common but inconspicuous bird. It creeps like a mouse, with jerky movements. It inhabits woods and shrubberies and feeds on insects. Most territories are held by a pair of birds, but sometimes a second male assists, or the male attracts additional females. A neat nest is built in a hedge or bush. The 4–6 eggs hatch after 12 days and young fly after 11 days. There are 2 or 3 broods.

adult

juvenile

THRUSHES AND CHATS

14 cm

J	F	M	A	M	J
J	A	S	O	N	D

Robin
Erithacus rubecula

ID FACT FILE

SIZE: Sparrow-sized

ADULT: Plump, with short neck. Brown with red breast and face, and white belly

JUVENILE: Brown and speckled

BILL: Black and slim

IN FLIGHT: White under tail

VOICE: Fluty song, slower and sadder in autumn and winter

LOOKALIKES:
Dunnock (p.181), Redstart (p.185), Bullfinch (p.244), Chaffinch (p.234)

In parts of Europe Robins are shy woodland birds, elsewhere they may be quite tame and live in gardens. NE European Robins migrate and many winter around the Mediterranean. Robins feed on insects. A nest of grasses and leaves is built among tree-roots or in other sheltered positions. The 4–6 eggs hatch after 13 days, young fly 13 days later and are cared for by both parents for 16–24 days. There are 2 or 3 broods.

adult

juvenile

THRUSHES AND CHATS

16.5 cm

J	F	M	A	M	J
J	A	S	O	N	D

ID FACT FILE

Size: Larger than Robin

Adult: Rich brown upperparts, paler underparts, reddish tail, large eyes

Juvenile: Dark and light spots on back, dark spots on breast

Bill: Brown with pale base

In flight: Longer-winged and a stronger flier than Robin

Voice: Rich, varied, fluty song with deep *took-took* notes and occasional thin *seep-seep*

Lookalikes: Robin (p.182), Redstart (p.185)

Nightingale
Luscinia megarhynchos

A skulking bird, easier to hear than to see. It sings during the day in spring, but its song is most noticeable after dark. It feeds mainly on insects and lives in woods and thickets. A summer migrant to S and central Europe. Builds a nest on or near the ground. The 4 or 5 eggs hatch after 13 days. Young fly after 11 days. In autumn it returns to tropical Africa.

adult

juvenile

14.5 cm

| J | F | M | A | M | J |
| J | A | S | O | N | D |

Black Redstart
Phoenicurus ochruros

ID FACT FILE

Size: Similar to Robin

Male (summer): Dark grey, pale patch on wings, rust-red tail

Female: Paler than male

Winter and first summer male: May be similar to female

Bill: Fine, black

In flight: Robin-like action. Red tail and rump contrast with dark body

Voice: Fast warbling song followed by metallic rattle. Repetitive *tpip* call. Hard *tic-tic* alarm

Lookalikes: Redstart (p.185)

At home on remote rock-strewn mountainsides, or in busy town centres and sometimes industrial areas where it will sing from rooftops. A summer migrant to central Europe which winters in lower-lying and coastal areas. It is resident in the south. It feeds on insects and fruit, and nests in a hole or on a ledge. The 4–6 eggs hatch after 13 days and young fly after 12 days. There are 2 broods.

adult male

adult females

THRUSHES AND CHATS

14 cm

| J | F | M | A | M | J |
| J | A | S | O | N | D |

Redstart
Phoenicurus phoenicurus

ID FACT FILE

Size: Similar to Robin

Male (breeding): Red tail with black centre, reddish underparts, grey back, black face, white forehead

Female: Brown body, paler underparts, red tail

Bill: Fine, black

In flight: Agile. Tail looks only loosely connected! Will fly from perch to snatch a flying insect; sometimes hovers

Voice: Sweet song with mechanical jangle at end. Call *hooveet*

Lookalikes: Black Redstart (p.184), Nightingale (p.183)

Slimmer than a Robin, with flickering red tail. The Redstart is a summer migrant to open woodlands and parkland throughout Europe, wintering in Africa. In places it has moved into towns. It eats mainly insects which it finds on the ground or among the leaves and branches. Nesting in a hole in tree or, sometimes, a nestbox, it lays 5–7 eggs which hatch after 12 days. Young fly after 14 days. There are usually 2 broods.

adult male summer

adult females

THRUSHES AND CHATS

12.5 cm

| J | F | M | A | M | J |
| J | A | S | O | N | D |

Whinchat
Saxicola rubetra

A small summer migrant to central and N Europe which winters in tropical Africa. It feeds on insects and seeds and lives in open country with meadows or other grasslands, young plantations and railway or roadside verges. Regularly perches on the tops of small trees, posts and wires. Nests on the ground among vegetation. The 4–7 eggs hatch after 12 days. Young leave the nest after 12 days and fly 5–6 days later.

ID FACT FILE

Size: Smaller than Robin

All birds: Flattish head. Perches upright

Male: Stripe over eye, dark cheeks, white patches on wings, mottled back and crown, pinkish breast

Female: Paler and less well marked than male

Bill: Fine, black

In flight: Cross-shaped, wings rather long and pointed, white patches at base of tail

Voice: Call a sharp *tic-tic*

Lookalikes: Stonechat (p.187), Wheatear (p.188)

adult male

adult female

juvenile

adult female

12.5 cm

| J | F | M | A | M | J |
| A | S | O | N | D | |

Stonechat
Saxicola torquata

ID FACT FILE

Size: Smaller than Robin

All birds: Short tail, plump, round head. Nervous actions

Male (breeding): Blackish head, white on neck, orange-red breast

Female: Lacks bold pattern of male

Bill: Small, black

In flight: Whirring, short, rounded wings, white shoulder patch, pale rump. Sometimes hovers

Voice: Hard *tac-tac*, like stones being struck together

Lookalikes: Whinchat (p.186)

Stonechats require grassy areas for feeding, dense cover (often gorse) for nesting and suitable perches or song-posts. They eat insects. The Stonechat is migratory in parts of Europe, resident in others, with additional visitors in winter. It nests close to the ground. The 4–6 eggs hatch after 13 days. Young fly at 13 days and depend on both parents for a few days, then only on the male as the female prepares for another brood. There are 2 or 3 broods.

adult male summer

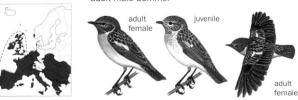

adult female

juvenile

adult female

14.5–15.5 cm

| J | F | M | A | M | J |
| J | A | S | O | N | D |

Wheatear
Oenanthe oenanthe

ID FACT FILE

SIZE: Slightly larger than Robin

ALL BIRDS: White rump, short black tail. Perches upright and flicks tail

MALE (BREEDING): Black cheeks, sandy breast, blue-grey back

MALE (NON-BREEDING): Less well marked

FEMALE AND JUVENILE: Like 'washed-out' male, uniform buff-brown

BILL: Fine, black

IN FLIGHT: White rump, black tail, sometimes hovers

VOICE: Scratchy song. Harsh *chack* call

LOOKALIKES: Whinchat (p.186)

A long-distance migrant from Africa to Europe; some travel even further afield, to Greenland or Siberia. Breeds in open country with bare areas such as rocky slopes, scree, tundra, cliff-tops, moors and dunes. Migrating Wheatears visit beaches and areas of short grass. The birds nest in holes, crevices or burrows. The 4–7 eggs hatch after 13 days. Young leave the nest at 10 days and fly at 15 days. There are 1 or 2 broods.

adult male breeding plumage

adult females

THRUSHES AND CHATS

23–24 cm

J	F	M	A	M	J
J	A	S	O	N	D

Ring Ouzel
Turdus torquatus

ID FACT FILE

Size: Slightly smaller than Blackbird

Male (W Europe): Sooty-black, pale crescent on breast, pale patch on wings

Male (E Europe): Paler, with bolder white wing patch, very scaly-looking

Female: Browner, less obvious crescent, scaly-looking

Juvenile: Lacks crescent mark. Greyer than Blackbird

Bill: Orange-yellow, dark tip

In flight: Rapid and direct

Voice: Fluty song. Call a loud rattling *tac,tac,tac*

Lookalikes: Blackbird (p.190)

A mountain blackbird. Found in summer on open moors, crags, gullies and boulder scree. In autumn it migrates to N Africa, but some remain around the Mediterranean. It feeds on insects, worms and berries. Nests in low vegetation, on a rock ledge or, in E Europe, in conifer trees. The 4 eggs hatch after 12 days. Young fly at 14 days and remain with parents for a further week or two. There are 1 or 2 broods.

adult male summer

adult female

juvenile

THRUSHES AND CHATS

24–25 cm

J	F	M	A	M	J
J	A	S	O	N	D

Blackbird

Turdus merula

ID FACT FILE

SIZE: Larger than Song Thrush

MALE: All black, with yellow eye-ring

FEMALE: Dark brown, pale chin, some spotting on breast

JUVENILE: Reddish-brown, with spotting on upperparts and breast

BILL: Male's yellow, female's brown

IN FLIGHT: Rapid, sometimes glides

VOICE: Clear and fluty song which tails off at the end. Loud chucking alarm call

LOOKALIKES: Ring Ouzel (p.189)

Some actions of a Blackbird are particularly characteristic, such as raising its tail on landing or turning over dead leaves under trees and shrubs as it searches for worms and other invertebrates. It also eats fruit, especially berries. The nest is built in a tree or bush. Between 3 and 5 eggs hatch after 13 days. Young fly after 13 days and are fed by parents for 3 weeks. There are 2 or 3 broods. Northern Blackbirds migrate south or west in autumn.

adult male

adult female   juvenile

THRUSHES AND CHATS

25.5 cm

J	F	M	A	M	J
J	A	S	O	N	D

Fieldfare
Turdus pilaris

ID FACT FILE

SIZE: Slightly larger than Blackbird

ALL BIRDS: Chestnut back, dark tail, grey head and rump, bold spots on yellowish breast

BILL: Yellow, dark tip in winter

IN FLIGHT: White underwing. Burst of wing-beats followed by glides

VOICE: Chuckling song, loud *chack-chack* call often given in flight

LOOKALIKES: Mistle Thrush (p.194)

A large thrush of northern woodlands of birch or conifers, but frequently moves away into open places. It has, in places, moved into towns. Feeds on invertebrates and fruits. It winters in central and S Europe and gathers into flocks. Nests in a tree, close to the trunk, laying 5 or 6 eggs which hatch after 10 days. Young fly after 12 days but depend on parents for a further 3 or 4 weeks. There are 2 broods.

adult

adult

23 cm

| J | F | M | A | M | J |
| J | A | S | O | N | D |

Song Thrush
Turdus philomelos

ID FACT FILE

SIZE: Smaller than Blackbird

ADULT: Rather short tail, brown above, pale below with many small spots

JUVENILE: Buff spots on back and head

BILL: Dark brown, yellow base

IN FLIGHT: Orange underwing, rapid and direct flight

VOICE: Song is made up of loud often fluty notes repeated several times then changed for other notes. Call is a sharp *sipp*

LOOKALIKES: Mistle Thrush (p.194), Redwing (p.193)

Many species eat snails, but only the Song Thrush methodically hammers open the larger ones, often using the same stone or other hard object. It also eats other invertebrates and fruits. It lives where there are trees or bushes and open grassland. A summer migrant to N Europe, resident or winter migrant elsewhere. Nests in trees and shrubs. The 3–5 egg hatch after 13 days and young fly 13 days later There are 2 or 3 broods.

adult

juvenile

adult

21 cm

| J | F | M | A | M | J |
| J | A | S | O | N | D |

ID FACT FILE

Size: Slightly smaller than Song Thrush

All birds: Darker than Song Thrush, white stripe over eye, reddish flanks

Bill: Dark, yellowish base

In flight: Red under wing

Voice: Song is loud fluty notes followed by rapid twittering. Call is urgent *tseep*, often given in flight

Lookalikes: Song Thrush (p.192)

Redwing
Turdus iliacus

This small thrush of northern woodlands migrates southwest in autumn. Often migrates after dark, and the high-pitched contact call can be heard as flocks fly overhead. In winter it feeds on berries or searches for worms on areas of short grass. It is vulnerable to extreme cold and will move to find milder feeding conditions in cold weather. The nest is on the ground or in a bush. The 4–6 eggs hatch after 12 days and young fly 10 days later. There are 2 broods.

adult

adult

27 cm

| J | F | M | A | M | J |
| J | A | S | O | N | D |

Mistle Thrush
Turdus viscivorus

ID FACT FILE

Size: The largest common thrush

Adults: Larger and greyer than Song Thrush. Rather small head, pale breast with large spots, white tips to outer tail feathers

Juvenile: Spotted upperparts

Bill: Dark

In flight: Powerful, direct. White underwing

Voice: Loud, clear, with fewer notes than Blackbird. Often sings in stormy conditions. Call is a chattering rattle

Lookalikes: Fieldfare (p.191), Song Thrush (p.192)

This bulky, upright thrush defends a large breeding territory in open woodland or parkland, but forms flocks in late summer. Northern populations are migratory. It eats invertebrates and fruits. In winter individuals sometimes defend a particularly good food supply such as a tree with berries. Nests early in the year, in a tree. The 3–5 eggs hatch after 12 days and young fly 12 days later. There are 2 broods.

adult

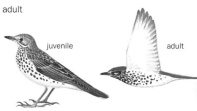

juvenile

adult

13.5 cm

| J | F | M | A | M | J |
| J | A | S | O | N | D |

Cetti's Warbler
Cettia cetti

ID FACT FILE

SIZE: Slightly smaller than House Sparrow

ALL BIRDS: Rather like large Wren: reddish-brown, paler underparts, pale stripe over eye, broad rounded tail which is often cocked up

BILL: Fine, dark

IN FLIGHT: Rapid, dashing from bush to bush

VOICE: Sudden loud bursts of rapid song

LOOKALIKES: Reed Warbler (p.198), Sedge Warbler (p.197)

This S European species has spread north recently. It is secretive, but has a distinctive song. Feeds on insects. Mainly resident and populations may fall after severe winters. Lives in dense bushes in marshes or near rivers. Males may have up to 4 different mates. Nests off the ground among vegetation. The 4–5 eggs hatch after 16 days. Young fly after 14 days and stay with parents for up to a month. There are 2 broods.

adult

adult

12.5 cm

J	F	M	A	M	J
J	A	S	O	N	D

Grasshopper Warbler
Locustella naevia

ID FACT FILE

Size: Smaller than House Sparrow

All birds: Faint stripe over eye, brown streaked upperparts, paler underparts, rounded tail

Bill: Fine, dark, with yellowish base

In flight: Rounded tail sometimes obvious

Voice: Insect-like reeling song continues for a minute or more without a break

Lookalikes: Cetti's Warbler (p.195), Sedge Warbler (p.197)

The Grasshopper Warbler's reeling song may be heard by day or night, but catching sight of this elusive species is difficult as it moves around in dense cover. It makes long unbroken flights to winter in Africa. Its summer home is meadowland, young plantations or fringes of wetlands. It eats insects, and builds a nest on or near the ground. The 5 or 6 eggs hatch after 12 days and young fly after 10–12 days. There are 2 broods.

adult

adult

13 cm

| J | F | M | A | M | J |
| J | A | S | O | N | D |

Sedge Warbler
Acrocephalus schoenobaenus

ID FACT FILE

Size: Smaller than House Sparrow

All birds: Streaked upper-parts, paler underparts, yellowish rump, white stripe over eye, dark crown

Bill: Blackish, with yellow base

In flight: Flits among vegetation. Song often given in short display flight

Voice: Song very varied with hard grating notes, and sparrow-like chirps

Lookalikes: Reed Warbler (p.198), Whitethroat (p.201)

A summer visitor chiefly to dense vegetation growing near lakes and rivers, where it feeds on insects. In autumn it returns to central or southern Africa, making a remarkable non-stop flight across both the Mediterranean and the Sahara. The nest is usually supported by growing vegetation less than 50cm from the ground. The 5 or 6 eggs hatch after 13 days. Young fly after 13 days. There are 1 or 2 broods.

adult

adult

WARBLERS AND CRESTS

13 cm

J	F	M	A	M	J
J	A	S	O	N	D

Reed Warbler
Acrocephalus scirpaceus

ID FACT FILE

Size: Smaller than House Sparrow

All birds: Plain brown upperparts, paler underparts, orangeish rump, steep forehead

Bill: Long, dark, pale base

In flight: Direct over reeds

Voice: Harsh churring, repetitive, with less variety than Sedge Warbler

Lookalikes: Sedge Warbler (p.197), Garden Warbler (p.202), Cetti's Warbler (p.195)

A summer visitor to stands of reeds around lakes or along rivers in many parts of Europe. It feeds on insects and spiders. Nests are woven around the stems of plants, especially common reed, usually over water. Dense, wet reedbeds may be home to large numbers of these birds. The 3–5 eggs hatch in 9–12 days. The young fly after 10 days and stay with parents for about 2 weeks. There are 1 or 2 broods. In autumn Reed Warblers return to central Africa.

adult

adult

12.5 cm

| J | F | M | A | M | J |
| A | S | O | N | D |

Dartford Warbler
Sylvia undata

ID FACT FILE

SIZE: Slightly larger than Blue Tit

ALL BIRDS: Domed head, long tail which may be cocked above back

MALE: Dark grey upperparts, rich reddish under-parts, pale spots on throat

FEMALE AND JUVENILE: Paler than male

BILL: Fine, brown, pale base

IN FLIGHT: Weak-looking. Tail appears disjointed

VOICE: Short repeated warble. Call is hard *tac*

LOOKALIKES: Whitethroat (p.201)

Small, long-tailed warbler living on lowland heaths with heather and gorse, but also in low bushes or open pine woods in SW Europe. The British population and some Continental birds are mainly resident, but there is some migration around the Mediterranean. Eats insects and spiders. A cup-shaped nest is built in low vegetation. The 3–5 eggs hatch after 12 days. Young fly at 12 days and are independent 2 weeks later. There are 2 or 3 broods.

adult

adult

12.5–13.5 cm

J	F	M	A	M	J
J	A	S	O	N	D

Lesser Whitethroat
Sylvia curruca

ID FACT FILE

SIZE: Slightly smaller than Whitethroat

ALL BIRDS: Grey-brown above, pale below, white throat, grey head with dark cheeks

BILL: Small, dark

IN FLIGHT: Rather compact. Direct between trees

VOICE: Call is sharp *tacc*. Song is a very quiet warble followed by dry rattle

LOOKALIKES: Whitethroat (p.201)

A rather unobtrusive warbler which sings only for a short season. It nests in hedges, bushes and small woodlands with dense cover. It feeds on insects and also berries in late summer. It winters mainly in NE Africa, making long non-stop southeastern flights with traditional stopping areas. It returns by a different route. The birds nest in small bushes. The 4–6 eggs hatch after 10 days and young fly 10 days later.

adult

adult

WARBLERS AND CRESTS

14 cm

| J | F | M | A | M | J |
| J | A | S | O | N | D |

Whitethroat
Sylvia communis

ID FACT FILE

Size: Similar to Great Tit

Male: White throat, grey head, reddish-brown wings, pale pink or grey breast

Female: Browner than male

Bill: Small, grey

In flight: White edges to tail Song-flight

Voice: Call a hard *tacc*. Song an unmusical jumble of notes

Lookalikes: Lesser Whitethroat (p.200)

A summer visitor to low, dense cover such as hedges or young plantations with patches of bramble or rose. It announces its presence with a scratchy song and a parachuting song-flight. It feeds mainly on insects. It migrates to the Sahel region of N Africa. Builds a cup-shaped nest in low bushes. The 4 or 5 eggs hatch after 11 days. Young fly after 10 days and stay with parents for 2 weeks.

adult male

adult male   adult female

WARBLERS AND CRESTS

14 cm

| J | F | M | A | M | J |
| J | A | S | O | N | D |

Garden Warbler
Sylvia borin

ID FACT FILE

SIZE: Slightly smaller than House Sparrow

ALL BIRDS: Plain brown upperparts, paler underparts, gentle face, no obvious marks

BILL: Short, strong-looking, brownish

IN FLIGHT: Direct. Square end to tail

VOICE: Steady stream of melodious phrases. Call *check-check*

LOOKALIKES: Blackcap (p.203), Reed Warbler (p.198), Chiffchaff (p.205)

Woodland edge, where the undergrowth is thickest, is the summer home of this very plain, rather retiring warbler with a lovely song. It feeds on insects in summer and fruits at other times. It winters in central and southern Africa. The cup-shaped nest is built in low bushes. Its 4 or 5 eggs hatch after 11 days and young fly at 10 days, staying with parents for 2 weeks after leaving the nest.

adult

adult

13 cm

J	F	M	A	M	J
J	A	S	O	N	D

Blackcap
Sylvia atricapilla

ID FACT FILE

SIZE: Slightly smaller than House Sparrow

MALE: Black crown, grey body, browner wings, pale underparts

FEMALE: Grey-brown, chestnut cap

BILL: Blackish, small

IN FLIGHT: Direct. Squared-off tail

VOICE: Clear, rich fluty song, more varied than Garden Warbler's

LOOKALIKES: Garden Warbler (p.202), Whitethroat (p.201)

The song of the Blackcap is a beautiful addition to mature woodlands and thickets. This warbler eats insects and fruits. In parts of W Europe the summer population migrates south to winter around the Mediterranean, and other Blackcaps from the east arrive. Sometimes these wintering birds visit gardens and bird tables. Blackcaps nest low down in dense vegetation. They lay 4–6 eggs which hatch after 11 days. Young fly at about 11 days. There are 1 or 2 broods.

adult male

adult male   adult female

12 cm

J	F	M	A	M	J
J	A	S	O	N	D

ID FACT FILE

SIZE: Slightly larger than Willow Warbler

ADULT: Yellow-green upper-parts, yellow breast sharply divided from pure white belly, yellow stripe over eye

JUVENILE: Duller

BILL: Large, brown, pale base

IN FLIGHT: Rather long wings and short tail. Hovers and has slow display flight

VOICE: Single attractive *vit* note repeated and getting faster and ending in trill. Plaintive *pew* call

LOOKALIKES: Willow Warbler (p.206), Chiff-chaff (p.205)

Wood Warbler
Phylloscopus sibilatrix

Mature woods with little undergrowth are the summer home of this rather smart warbler. It has an attractive song and a slow, butterfly-like display flight. It feeds on insects and frequently hovers to pick food from the undersides of leaves. In autumn it migrates to central Africa. It builds a domed nest on the ground, laying 5–7 eggs which hatch after 12 days. Young fly after 12 days and stay with parents for a month

adult summer

adult spring

juvenile

10–11 cm

J	F	M	A	M	J
J	A	S	O	N	D

Chiffchaff
Phylloscopus collybita

ID FACT FILE

Size: Smaller than Blue Tit

Adult: Brown above, pale yellowish-brown below, faint stripe over eye, dark legs. More rounded head and longer tail than Willow Warbler

Juvenile: Tends to be more yellow than adult

Bill: Black, blunt

In flight: Shorter, more rounded wings than Willow Warbler

Voice: Song a repetitive *zip-zap, zip-zap.* Call a single plaintive *weet*

Lookalikes: Willow Warbler (p.206), Wood Warbler (p.204)

A summer visitor to woods and copses over most of Europe, best known for its simple repetitive song. In autumn Chiffchaffs migrate south and west to winter around the Mediterranean and in other milder areas. Feeds on insects which it finds in trees and bushes and sometimes catches in flight. Nests in vegetation on or near the ground, laying 4–7 eggs which hatch after 13 days. Young fly at 16 days. There are 2 broods.

adult summer

adult spring

WARBLERS AND CRESTS

10.5–11.5 cm

| J | F | M | A | M | J |
| J | A | S | O | N | D |

Willow Warbler
Phylloscopus trochilus

ID FACT FILE

Size: Smaller than Blue Tit

All birds: Like Chiffchaff, with different song, pale legs, slim rear body

Adult: Brown-green upperparts, yellowish under-parts, pale stripe over eye. Brighter in autumn

Juvenile: Bright yellow underparts

Bill: Long, brown

In flight: Longer wings and tail than Chiffchaff, sometimes hovers

Voice: Sweet-sounding, trickling down a scale. Call is a slightly drawn-out *hooet*

Lookalikes: Chiff-chaff (p.205), Wood Warbler (p.204)

Europe's most numerous summer migrant, which winters in central and southern Africa – for some birds a journey of 12,000 km. It feeds on insects, spiders and berries. Males return first in spring and take up territory in northern birch woods, scrub, woodland edges and bushes in open country. Nests among vegetation on the ground. The 4–8 eggs hatch after 12 days. Young fly at 12 days and depend on parents for a further 2 weeks.

adult summer

adult spring

juvenile

WARBLERS AND CRESTS

9 cm

| J | F | M | A | M | J |
| J | A | S | O | N | D |

Goldcrest
Regulus regulus

ID FACT FILE

Size: Smaller than Wren

Male: Greenish with paler underparts. Dumpy with short tail. Two small wingbars, yellow and orange crown stripe, pale face and large dark eye

Juvenile: No crown stripe

Bill: Dark, small, pointed

In flight: Tiny, rapid flight on rounded wings. Short tail. Flits among branches, briefly hovers

Voice: Call a thin *see*. Song a thin rising and falling trill

Lookalikes: Firecrest (p.208), Willow Warbler (p.206)

The smallest European bird. It flits restlessly from branch to branch. It breeds in conifer woods, in evergreens in parks and sometimes in deciduous woodland. After nesting, Goldcrests join flocks of small birds and may visit other habitats. Northern goldcrests migrate south to central and S Europe. The birds eat insects and spiders. The nest hangs from thin branches, and the 9–11 eggs hatch after 16 days. Young fly at 19 days. There are 2 broods.

adult

juvenile

WARBLERS AND CRESTS

9 cm

| J | F | M | A | M | J |
| J | A | S | O | N | D |

Firecrest
Regulus ignicapillus

ID FACT FILE

Size: Marginally larger than Goldcrest

All birds: Cleaner, brighter, more boldly marked than Goldcrest. Orange crown, white stripe over eye, greenish upperparts, paler underparts, orangeish shoulders

Bill: Short, pointed, black

In flight: Active, restless

Voice: Less high-pitched than Goldcrest, less varied song. *Zit* call

Lookalikes: Goldcrest (p.207)

This tiny bird has a more southerly distribution than Goldcrest, but both occur together in many localities. The Firecrest nests in conifers or sometimes in other trees, often feeding in dense undergrowth and visiting low bushes. It migrates southwest in autumn. Feeds on insects. A beautiful cup-shaped nest is suspended from a small branch. The 7–12 eggs hatch after 15 days. Young fly at about 22 days. There are 2 broods.

adult

juvenile

FLYCATCHERS

14.5 cm

J	F	M	A	M	J
J	A	S	O	N	D

Spotted Flycatcher
Muscicapa striata

ID FACT FILE

Size: Slightly smaller than House Sparrow

Adult: Upright stance, grey-brown back, pale streaked underparts, streaked forehead and crown

Juvenile: Buffer than adult, with spotted head, back and breast

Bill: Dark, broad base

In flight: Swoops after flies, flits from perch to perch

Voice: Quiet warbling song. Call is a thin squeaking *teeeze* or harder *tees-tuk-tuk*

Lookalikes: Dunnock (p.181), Tree Pipit (p.171)

A master of flight. Darts from a perch to snatch an insect from the air and lands with a flick of its wings. A summer migrant to woodland glades and gardens with mature trees, this flycatcher winters in southern Africa. It nests in a cavity or among vegetation against a tree-trunk or wall. The 4–6 eggs hatch after 13 days. Young fly 13 days later and may depend on parents for a month. There are 1 or 2 broods.

juvenile

adult

FLYCATCHERS

13 cm

| J | F | M | A | M | J |
| J | A | S | O | N | D |

Pied Flycatcher
Ficedula hypoleuca

ID FACT FILE

Size: Smaller than Spotted Flycatcher

All birds: Round head. Flicks wings, wags tail

Male (spring): Black above, white below, white patch on wing, white spot above bill

Male (autumn): Similar to female

Female: Brown and white, white wing-patch

Bill: Short, black

In flight: White wing-bar

Voice: Sweet-sounding warble. Call a sharp *tac* or *wheeet*

Lookalikes: Pied Wagtail (p.177), Spotted Flycatcher (p.209)

The small plump flycatcher is a summer migrant to mainly mature deciduous woods with open areas and suitable holes for nesting. It has been attracted to some woods by nestboxes. Feeds on insects, many of which it chases and catches in mid-air. Autumn migrants fly to Portugal or Spain and feed up before flying direct to W Africa. Lays 6 or 7 eggs which hatch after 13 days. Young fly after 14 days.

adult male spring

adult female

TITS AND ALLIES

16.5 cm

J	F	M	A	M	J
J	A	S	O	N	D

Bearded Tit
Panurus biarmicus

ID FACT FILE

SIZE: Great Tit-sized with longer tail

ALL BIRDS: A similar colour to dead reeds, long-tailed

MALE: Blue-grey head, black moustache, delicate wing-pattern

FEMALE: Lacks head-pattern of male but has similar wing-pattern

BILL: Tiny, orange

IN FLIGHT: Rather weak. Whirring wings. Flies over tops of reeds. Long broad tail very obvious

VOICE: Loud *ching-ching* call

LOOKALIKES: None in area

An elusive species living in dense reed-beds where it feeds on insects, especially the larvae of moths, also spiders and seeds. It is mainly resident, but young birds roam more widely in winter. In some years, when numbers have built up, it 'erupts' and spreads to new areas. Severe winter weather can drastically reduce populations. Nests are built among reeds, and 4–8 eggs hatch after 11 days. Young fly after 12 days. There are 2–4 broods.

adult male

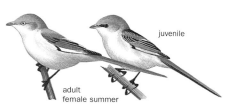

juvenile

adult
female summer

TITS AND ALLIES

14 cm

J	F	M	A	M	J
J	A	S	O	N	D

Long-tailed Tit
Aegithalos caudatus

ID FACT FILE

Size: Goldcrest-sized body, tail longer than body

Adult: Black and white, with variable amount of reddish-brown

Northern birds: White head

Juvenile: Shorter tail, browner, variable head-pattern

Bill: Short, stubby

In flight: Weak-looking, undulating. Obvious long tail

Voice: High-pitched *seee-seee*, low trilling *triupp*

Lookalikes: Pied Wagtail (p.177)

Tiny body and very long tail. Mainly resident in scrub and woodland edges and visits parks and gardens. Outside the breeding season family groups roam widely and often join other families, forming flocks of over 20. At night they roost communally. The beautiful domed nest is built of moss, lichen and spiders' webs. The 8–12 eggs hatch after 15 days. Other adults may assist parents to feed their young, which fly after 14 days.

adult

juvenile

adult
northern europe

TITS AND ALLIES

11.5 cm

J	F	M	A	M	J
J	A	S	O	N	D

Crested Tit
Parus cristatus

ID FACT FILE

SIZE: Similar to Blue Tit

ALL BIRDS: Rather plump with large head, black and white face and crest, brown back, pale under-parts

BILL: Black

IN FLIGHT: Rather strong and bouncy

VOICE: Call a purring trill *zee-zee-zee*

LOOKALIKES: Coal Tit (p.216), Blue Tit (p. 217)

A forest species living mainly in pine woods but in some deciduous woods in S Europe. Searches among the highest branches for insects and spiders, but also feeds lower down and may come close to an observer. It is resident throughout the year, although juveniles sometimes rove further afield. Nests in holes in trees. The 6 or 7 eggs hatch after 13 days. Young fly after 18 days and stay with parents for about 3 weeks.

adult

juvenile

11.5 cm

| J | F | M | A | M | J |
| J | A | S | O | N | D |

ID FACT FILE

Size: Similar to Blue Tit

All birds: Large head, pale wing-panel, dull black crown, square-ended tail. Larger black bib than Marsh Tit, and often looks fluffier

Scandinavian birds: Grey and white body

Southern races: Brown back, off-white underparts

Bill: Small, black

In flight: Flitting; may look weaker than Marsh Tit

Voice: Piping *piu-piu*, buzzing *ezz-ezz-ezz*

Lookalikes: Marsh Tit (p.215), Coal Tit, (p.216) Blackcap (p.203)

Willow Tit
Parus montanus

A similar-looking species to Marsh Tit. Resident over much of Europe, but migratory in the far north. In places it lives in conifer woods, elsewhere in deciduous woods, especially wet woodlands with willow and alder. It eats insects and seeds. The usual nest site is a hole excavated in a rotten tree-stump. The clutch size may be influenced by the size of the cavity. The 4–11 eggs hatch after 13 days, and the young fly after 17 days.

adult

juvenile

11.5 cm

TITS AND ALLIES

J	F	M	A	M	J
J	A	S	O	N	D

Marsh Tit
Parus palustris

ID FACT FILE

Size: Similar to Blue Tit

All birds: Glossy black cap, white cheeks, small black bib, plain brown back and wings, pale underparts, slightly forked tail

Bill: Short, black

In flight: Appears stronger than Blue Tit

Voice: Explosive *pit-chu* call is typical, also harsh *tcharr-tcharr*

Lookalikes: Willow Tit (p.214), Coal Tit (p.216), Blackcap (p.203)

A resident of deciduous woodland in central Europe. Rather secretive. It eats insects, spiders, fruits and seeds, feeding among the leaves or taking food from the ground. In autumn it joins roaming flocks of other small birds such as Blue Tits. It sometimes visits bird tables and often stores food which it hides and may retrieve again later. Nests in a hole in a tree, a stump, a wall or among roots. The 7–10 eggs hatch after 13 days. Young fly at 17 days.

adult

juvenile

11.5 cm

J	F	M	A	M	J
J	A	S	O	N	D

Coal Tit
Parus ater

ID FACT FILE

Size: Similar to Blue Tit

Adults: Blue-grey, black head with white checks, white stripe on back of head, small double wing-bar, short tail

Juvenile: Yellowish underparts and cheeks

Bill: Quite long, pointed

In flight: Very rapid, sometimes hovers. Has short tail and wing-bars

Voice: Fast, shrill *teach-tu, teach-tu*

Lookalikes: Marsh Tit (p.215), Willow Tit (p.214), Great Tit (p.218)

Conifer woods are the usual home for this small bird. Resident in S and W Europe but migratory elsewhere. Large-scale movements are sometimes triggered by shortage of food. In autumn and winter it may join flocks of other small birds and visit a variety of habitats including gardens. Eats insects, spiders and seeds. Nests in holes, including underground. The 8–9 eggs hatch after 14 days. Young fly after 19 days. There are 1 or 2 broods.

adult

juvenile

TITS AND ALLIES

11.5 cm

J	F	M	A	M	J
J	A	S	O	N	D

Blue Tit
Parus caeruleus

ID FACT FILE

Size: Smaller than House Sparrow

Adult: Blue and green back, yellow under-parts, white cheeks and blue crown

Juvenile: Like parents but less colourful, with yellow cheeks

Bill: Small and dark

In flight: Small with rounded wings

Voice: Call a shrill *tsee-tsee-tsee*

Lookalikes: Great Tit (p.218), Crested Tit (p.213)

A resident woodland species. In summer it lives in lowland habitats where there are mature deciduous trees with suitable nest-holes. Will also visit other habitats, such as gardens and reed-beds, especially in winter. Feeds on insects, fruits and seeds. Breeds during April or May. A nest of moss and grasses is built in a hole in a tree, or in a nestbox. Between 6 and 16 eggs hatch after 14 days and young fly 16–22 days later. There is usually 1 brood.

adult

juvenile

14 cm

| J | F | M | A | M | J |
| J | A | S | O | N | D |

Great Tit
Parus major

ID FACT FILE

SIZE: Sparrow-sized

ALL BIRDS: Black head, white cheeks, yellow underparts

MALE: Broader black stripe on belly than female

BILL: Strong, dark grey

JUVENILE: Paler version of adult

IN FLIGHT: White outer tail feathers, white wing-bar

VOICE: Loud repetitive *tee-cher, tee-cher*

LOOKALIKES: Blue Tit (p.217), Coal Tit (p.216)

Lowland deciduous forest is the Great Tit's natural home, but it may breed in more open habitats with a scattering of large trees. Visits other habitats outside the nesting season. Come to gardens for food and will sometimes nest. Feeds on insects, seeds and nuts. Nests in holes in trees and uses nestboxes. Between 3 and 18 eggs are laid in April or May. Young hatch after 14 days and leave the nest about 18 days later. There is usually 1 brood, but occasionally 2.

adult male

juvenile

14 cm

| J | F | M | A | M | J |
| J | A | S | O | N | D |

Nuthatch

Sitta europaea

ID FACT FILE

Size: Similar to Great Tit

All birds: Large head, short tail, blue-grey back, buff underparts, thick black line through eye

Bill: Long, stout, pointed

In flight: Pointed head, short square tail, broad rounded wings

Voice: Call a short loud *tuit,tuit*. Song a fast rattling *pee-pee-pee-pee*

Lookalikes: Lesser Spotted Woodpecker (p.164), Great Tit (p.218)

Resident in deciduous woodland over much of Europe and, less frequently, in pine woods. On tree-trunks and branches it moves with little jumps and often descends head-first. It eats insects and seeds, including nuts which it wedges in a crevice and hammers open. Nests in holes and plasters the entrance with mud to deter other species from entering. The 6–8 eggs hatch after 14 days. Young fly after 23 days.

adult

adult male
Northern Europe

adult female
Western Europe

12.5 cm

J	F	M	A	M	J
J	A	S	O	N	D

Treecreeper
Certhia familiaris

Small brown woodland bird which creeps like a mouse up tree-trunks and larger branches, usually spiralling round as it searches for insects and spiders and some seeds in winter. Mainly resident, but some northern tree-creepers migrate. At night treecreepers roost in crevices in tree-trunks, especially ornamental redwoods. The nest is built in a crevice, often behind loose bark. The 5 or 6 eggs hatch after 14 days and the young fly after 15 days. There are 1 or 2 broods.

ID FACT FILE

SIZE: Smaller than Nuthatch

ALL BIRDS: Brown stripy back, white underparts, ragged stripe over eye, stiff pointed tail feathers

BILL: Long, down-curved

IN FLIGHT: Fluttering, butterfly-like. Swoops from top of one trunk to bottom of next. Broad orange wing-bar

VOICE: High-pitched *tsee, tsee* call. Song a high-pitched series of notes ending in a flourish

LOOKALIKES: None in area

adult

adult

24 cm

| J | F | M | A | M | J |
| J | A | S | O | N | D |

Golden Oriole
Oriolus oriolus

ID FACT FILE

SIZE: Similar to Blackbird

MALE: Yellow, with black wings and central tail

FEMALE AND JUVENILE: Yellowish-green, dark wings, pale and streaked underparts

BILL: Long, heavy, deep pink

IN FLIGHT: Thrush-like. Closes wings and sweeps up to land on a perch

VOICE: Clear and flutey *weela-wheeloo*

LOOKALIKES: Green Woodpecker (p.162)

One of Europe's most attractive summer visitors with both beautiful plumage and a melodious song. It winters in central and southern Africa and returns in spring to nest in lowland woods and other areas of deciduous trees such as poplar plantations. It feeds on insects and berries. The delicately woven nest is built in a fork of a branch high in the tree-tops. The eggs hatch after 16 days and young fly at 16 days.

adult male

adult male   adult female   juvenile

SHRIKES

17 cm

Red-backed Shrike
Lanius collurio

ID FACT FILE

SIZE: Smaller than Starling

ALL BIRDS: White edges to long tail which is constantly moving from side to side or up and down

MALE: Reddish back, pink flush to breast, bluish head, black 'mask'

FEMALE: Duller, scaly breast

JUVENILE: Like female, with scaly upperparts

BILL: Hooked tip

IN FLIGHT: Direct over short distances, swooping over longer distances. Erratic chase after prey

VOICE: Harsh *chack-chack*

LOOKALIKES: None in area

A summer visitor from southern Africa. Feeds on large insects, such as grasshoppers, and also small birds, mammals and reptiles. Prey is frequently stored by spearing it on a thorn or barbed wire. Breeds in open country with low thorn bushes, often near woodland. Nests low in dense bushes. The 3–7 eggs hatch after 14 days. Young fly at 14 days and the family may stay around the nest site for a further month.

adult male summer

adult female

juvenile

SHRIKES

24–25 cm

| J | F | M | A | M | J |
| J | A | S | O | N | D |

Great Grey Shrike
Lanius excubitor

ID FACT FILE

Size: Similar to Blackbird

All birds: Grey with black mask, grey forehead, white streak over eye, black wings with a white bar, long tail with white edges

S Europe: Darker back, less white on wings, pinkish underparts

Bill: Black, strong, hooked tip

In flight: Fast, powerful, bounding. Drops to the ground or sweeps up to perch

Voice: Harsh chattering

Lookalikes: None in area

Widespread in open country where it perches on the tops of bushes, small trees or wires. It summers from the Arctic to the Mediterranean. Northern birds migrate and winter in other parts of Europe. Eats large insects, small mammals, birds and reptiles. The prey is sometimes impaled on thorns. The nest is in a fork of a tree, and the 4–7 eggs hatch after 15 days. Young fly at 15 days, but may leave the nest earlier.

adult

34–35 cm

J	F	M	A	M	J
J	A	S	O	N	D

Jay
Garrulus glandarius

ID FACT FILE

SIZE: Larger than town pigeon

ALL BIRDS: Pinkish-brown body, black and white wings with blue patch, black tail, white rump, small grey and white crest (sometimes raised)

OTHER RACES: Some variation in colours

BILL: Heavy, dark

IN FLIGHT: Rowing motion on broad, rounded wings. Blue wing-patch, white rump

VOICE: Wide range of calls including loud raucous screech

LOOKALIKES: None in area

A noisy but shy woodland species. Usually associated with deciduous woodland, but inhabits conifer woods in some places and also parks and large gardens. Eats invertebrates, seeds (especially acorns), eggs and young birds Mainly resident, but migratory in the north, and occasionally food shortages trigger large movements. Nests in a fork of a tree. The 5–7 eggs hatch after 16 days. Young fly at 21 days and are fed by parents for 8 weeks.

adult

adult

CROWS

44–46 cm

| J | F | M | A | M | J |
| J | A | S | O | N | D |

Magpie
Pica pica

ID FACT FILE

Size: Larger than Woodpigeon

Adult: Iridescent black and white, with long graduated tail

Juvenile: Shorter tail, white feathers look dirty

Bill: Strong, black

In flight: Broad rounded wings, long tail,

Voice: Harsh, chattering *chack-chack*, *chack*

Lookalikes: None in area

A familiar bird of open countryside with trees, farmland with hedges, woodland fringes, scrub and, increasingly, parks and gardens. Eats a wide range of food including insects, seeds, berries and carrion as well as small birds and eggs. A resident, but flocks together outside the breeding season. Builds a domed nest of sticks in a tree or tall bush. The 5–7 eggs hatch after 21 days. Young fly after 24 days and stay with parents for a month or more.

adult

adult

CROWS

39–40 cm

| J | F | M | A | M | J |
| J | A | S | O | N | D |

Chough
Pyrrhocorax pyrrhocorax

ID FACT FILE

SIZE: Larger than Jackdaw

ALL BIRDS: Glossy black, with red legs

BILL: Long, down-curved. Adult's red, juvenile's shorter and dull yellow

IN FLIGHT: Buoyant, acrobatic. Deeply fingered, broad wings, square-ended tail

VOICE: Ringing *chow*

LOOKALIKES: Jackdaw (p.227), Rook (p.228)

A red-billed crow of uplands and crags in S Europe and rocky sea-coasts in the west. It feeds on the ground in pastures and short grass on cliff-tops where it probes for invertebrates, and it also eats grain and berries. Mainly sedentary and usually in flocks. Very acrobatic, frequently swooping and diving. Nests in rock crevices, sometimes in buildings. The 3–5 eggs hatch after 17 days. Young fly at 31–41 days and stay with parents for 4–5 weeks.

adult

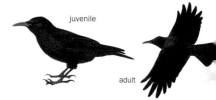

juvenile

adult

CROWS

33–34 cm

J	F	M	A	M	J
J	A	S	O	N	D

Jackdaw
Corvus monedula

ID FACT FILE

SIZE: Smaller than Rook

ALL BIRDS: Black, grey back of head, pale eye

BILL: Short, strong, black

IN FLIGHT: Acrobatic flight. Less fingered wings than other black crows. Can look pigeon-like

VOICE: sharp *jac*, ringing *key-ow*

LOOKALIKES: Chough (p.226), Rook (p.228)

Small black crow with patchy distribution. Colonial, living on farmland with livestock, on cliffs (including sea-cliffs), in woodland and in villages. Often mixes with Rooks and Starlings. Mainly a resident, except in N Europe. Eats a variety of food, including invertebrates, fruits, grain and eggs. Nests in holes in trees, cliffs and buildings. The 4–6 eggs hatch after 17 days. Young fly at 32 days and become independent after 5 weeks.

adult

adult

44–46 cm

J	F	M	A	M	J
J	A	S	O	N	D

Rook
Corvus frugilegus

ID FACT FILE

SIZE: Similar to Carrion Crow

ADULT: Glossy black plumage, greyish face, steep forehead, loose feathers at top of legs.

JUVENILE: Similar to adult with dark face

BILL: Long, pointed, pale base

IN FLIGHT: Fingered wing-tips, rounded tail. Narrower wings than Carrion Crow

VOICE: Harsh *karrr*

LOOKALIKES: Carrion Crow (p.229), Raven (p.230), Jackdaw (p.227)

Rookeries of tens, sometimes hundreds, of nests are usually built in the branches of tall trees. Northern populations migrate south and west in autumn. In winter flocks of hundreds of Rooks feed together and evening roosts may attract a thousand birds or more. Rooks feed on invertebrates, grain and carrion. The 2–6 eggs hatch after 16 days. Young fly after 30 days and continue to be fed by parents for 6 weeks.

adult

juvenile

adult

CROWS

45–47 cm

| F | M | A | M | J |
| A | S | O | N | D |

Carrion/Hooded Crow
Corvus corone

ID FACT FILE

SIZE: Similar to Rook

CARRION CROW: Heavy-looking, black

HOODED CROW: Grey or pinkish-brown body, black head, black tail and wings

IN FLIGHT: Powerful and slow. Fingered ends to wings

VOICE: Deep, rasping *kwarrr*

LOOKALIKES: Raven (p.230), Rook (p.228)

All-black Carrion Crows live in Asia and parts of W Europe, in between there are grey and black crows called Hooded Crows. Where races meet they often interbreed. This crow eats invertebrates, grain, small animals and carrion. It is migratory in the north, sedentary in the south. Carrion crows are less gregarious than Rooks, but flocks and communal roosts do occur. The nest of sticks is built in a tree. The 3–6 eggs hatch after 18 days and young fly after 32 days.

adult hybrid

adult Carrion

adult Hooded

immature Carrion (right)
adult Hooded (below)

arrion

Hooded

CROWS

64 cm

| J | F | M | A | M | J |
| J | A | S | O | N | D |

Raven
Corvus corax

ID FACT FILE

SIZE: Similar to Buzzard

ALL BIRDS: All-black, with shaggy throat feathers and rather flat head

BILL: Deep, black, powerful

IN FLIGHT: Cross-shaped. Wings are long, broad and fingered. Wedge-shaped tail. Often 'tumbles' and plays in the air

VOICE: Deep, hollow *prruk, prruk*

LOOKALIKES: Carrion Crow (p.229)

The largest crow lives in many habitats: sea-cliffs, mountain crags, upland moors and fores[t] edges. It sometimes kills animals and also eats carrion. Mostly resident, although northern birds move south in winter. Nesting starts as early as February, in a nest of sticks in a tree o[r] on a rock ledge. The 4–6 eggs hatch after 20 days. Young fly after 45 days and depend on their parents for over 4 months.

adult

adult

37–42 cm

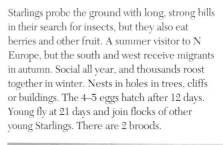

Starling
Sturnus vulgaris

ID FACT FILE

Size: Smaller than Blackbird

All birds: Oily greenish-black. Short tail

Adult (winter): Pale tips to feathers give spotted appearance to back and breast

Adult (summer): Appears black, less spotted

Juvenile: Brown, paler underparts, almost white chin

Bill: Long, yellow when breeding, otherwise brown

In flight: Fast, direct, with pointed triangular wings

Voice: Scratchy whistles and warbles

Lookalikes: Blackbird (p.190)

Starlings probe the ground with long, strong bills in their search for insects, but they also eat berries and other fruit. A summer visitor to N Europe, but the south and west receive migrants in autumn. Social all year, and thousands roost together in winter. Nests in holes in trees, cliffs or buildings. The 4–5 eggs hatch after 12 days. Young fly at 21 days and join flocks of other young Starlings. There are 2 broods.

adult summer

adult male winter   immature   juvenile

SPARROWS, BUNTINGS AND FINCHES

14–15 cm

| J | F | M | A | M | J |
| J | A | S | O | N | D |

ID FACT FILE

SIZE: Slightly larger than Tree Sparrow

MALE: Brown streaked upperparts, pale underparts, grey crown, black throat, pale cheeks, grey rump

FEMALE AND JUVENILE: Duller, without prominent head markings. Straw-coloured stripe behind eye

BILL: Short, stubby

IN FLIGHT: Bounding, whirring wings

VOICE: Loud *chirrup*

LOOKALIKES: Tree Sparrow (p.233)

House Sparrow
Passer domesticus

Originally from central Asia, the House Sparrow's association with man has taken it to ever continent except Antarctica. It eats grain and many other foods. A resident which flocks in autumn and winter where food is plentiful. Nests in holes, often in buildings, but sometimes builds an untidy, domed nest in a tree o bush. The 3–5 eggs hatch after 12 days. Young fly after 14 days and feed themselves 7 days later. There are 1–4 broods.

adult male spring

adult female

adult male winter

SPARROWS, BUNTINGS AND FINCHES

14 cm

| J | F | M | A | M | J |
| J | A | S | O | N | D |

Tree Sparrow
Passer montanus

ID FACT FILE

SIZE: Slightly smaller than House Sparrow

ALL BIRDS: All-brown crown, black spot on pale cheeks, small black bib, pale collar

BILL: Small, dark, strong

IN FLIGHT: Typical small bird, fast and agile

VOICE: Hard *tac-tac*

LOOKALIKES: House Sparrow (p.232), Reed Bunting (p.249)

Widespread in both Europe and Asia, but showing a recent decline in the British Isles. Mainly a resident, sometimes 'erupting' to populate a new area. Feeds on insects and plant material. Flocks in winter and often joins with other species. Found in open deciduous woodland and farmland. Nests in holes in cliffs, trees and buildings. The 5 eggs hatch after 11 days. Young fly after 15 days and are independent 2 weeks later. There are 1–3 broods.

adult

juvenile

14.5 cm

| J | F | M | A | M | J |
| J | A | S | O | N | D |

Chaffinch
Fringilla coelebs

ID FACT FILE

SIZE: Sparrow-sized

MALE: Pink breast and face, rest of head blue-grey. Two bold white wing-bars

FEMALE: Shades of grey-brown, white wing-bars

BILL: Blue-grey, short and thick

IN FLIGHT: White wing-bars and outer tail feathers very prominent

VOICE: Loud *tink*. Song a musical rattle with flourish at end

LOOKALIKES: Brambling (p.235), Bullfinch (p.244)

A familiar bird of woodland and other areas with trees in central and S Europe. Northern Chaffinches migrate in autumn, swelling numbers in the south and west. In autumn flocks gather with other species on farmland. The Chaffinch eats seeds and insects. It builds a neat nest of moss and lichen among branches or against a tree-trunk. The 4 or 5 eggs hatch after 12 days. Young fly at 14 days and depend on parents for 3 weeks.

adult male

adult females

14 cm

F M A M J
A S O N D

Brambling
Fringilla montifringilla

A summer migrant to northern birch forests
and other woodland, where it eats mainly
insects. A winter migrant to farmland and
woodland in central and S Europe, feeding on
seeds, especially beech mast. It flocks with
other small birds or forms its own flocks which
may be small or, occasionally, very large. The
cup-shaped nest of moss and lichen is built
against a tree-trunk or in a fork. The 5–7 eggs
hatch after 11 days. Young fly at 13 days.

adult male summer

adult male
summer

adult male
winter

adult female
summer

adult female
summer

SPARROWS, BUNTINGS AND FINCHES

15 cm

| J | F | M | A | M | J |
| J | A | S | O | N | D |

Greenfinch
Carduelis chloris

ID FACT FILE

SIZE: Similar to House Sparrow

MALE: Green, green-brown wings, yellow on wings and tail

FEMALE: Duller, streaked back, yellow on wings and tail

JUVENILE: Similar to female but heavily streaked

BILL: Strong, pale

IN FLIGHT: Yellow on wings and tail, green rump

VOICE: Twittering flight call. Twittering song ends with nasal *dwzeeeee*

LOOKALIKES: Siskin (p.238), Goldfinch (p.237), Crossbill (p.242)

Resident in most of Europe, but northern populations migrate. The Greenfinch's large bill allows it to open seeds of various sizes including peanuts hung up in gardens for tits. It breeds in loose colonies in woodland, parks and large gardens. In winter it is widespread and forms flocks in open areas including arable fields. A bulky nest is built in a thick shrub. The 4–6 eggs hatch after 13 days. Young fly 14 days. There are 2 broods.

adult male

adult female

adult female

juvenile

SPARROWS, BUNTINGS AND FINCHES

12 cm

| F | M | A | M | J |
| A | S | O | N | D |

Goldfinch
Carduelis carduelis

This beautiful small finch has a longer, more
pointed bill than that of the Greenfinch, and
uses it to extract seeds from food plants such as
thistles. It summers in lowland Europe where
there is open country with trees for nesting in.
In autumn many move south towards the
Mediterranean. The neat, deep nest is built
towards the end of a branch. The 4–6 eggs
hatch after 11 days and the young fly after 13
days. There are 1–3 broods.

adult

juvenile

adult

SPARROWS, BUNTINGS AND FINCHES

12 cm

Siskin
Carduelis spinus

ID FACT FILE

Size: Smaller than Greenfinch

All birds: Streaky yellowish-green, short forked tail, yellow in wings and tail

Male (spring): Black bib and crown

Male (winter): Head-pattern less distinct

Female: Greyer and more streak-ed than male

Bill: Short, point-ed. Male's is pale, others darker

In flight: Light, bouncy. Yellow on wings, tail and rump

Voice: Sweet twittering song. Call is clear *tsuu*

Lookalikes: Green-finch (p.236)

A small finch of conifer forests. In autumn it migrates, and flocks of Siskins are more wide-spread, feeding on birch and alder seeds and sometimes visiting gardens to take peanuts. They hang like tits to reach their food. Numb vary considerably from year to year. The nest small, compact and built out on a branch. The 3–5 eggs hatch after 12 days and the young fly after 13 days. There are 1 or 2 broods.

adult male

adult female

adu
fem

juvenile

SPARROWS, BUNTINGS AND FINCHES

13.5 cm

F	M	A	M	J
A	S	O	N	D

Linnet
Carduelis cannabina

Open countryside, farmland and lowland heath are home for the Linnet. It feeds almost exclusively on seeds of weeds and other plants. There is some migration and flocks form in winter, often joining with other small birds. Groups of Linnets often nest in close proximity. The nest of twigs, roots and moss is built in dense cover. The 4–6 eggs hatch after 11 days and young fly after 11 days. There are 2 or 3 broods.

D FACT FILE

ZE: Smaller than House Sparrow

ALL BIRDS: Short-tailed, brown above, paler below

MALE (SPRING): Red forehead, grey head, red breast, plain brown back

MALE (WINTER): Lacks red marks

FEMALE: More streaked than winter male

BILL: Grey, small

IN FLIGHT: Sparrow-like, white flashes In wings and tail

VOICE: Twittering and warbling song. Twittering flight call

LOOKALIKES: Red-poll (p.241), Twite (p.240)

adult male

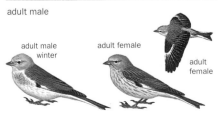

adult male winter

adult female

adult female

14 cm

J	F	M	A	M	J
J	A	S	O	N	D

Twite
Carduelis flavirostris

ID FACT FILE

SIZE: Similar to Linnet

ALL BIRDS: Longer, more forked tail than Linnet, with more stripy, darker upper-parts, pale wing-bar

MALE (SPRING): Pinkish rump

BILL: Grey in spring, yellowish at other times

IN FLIGHT: Similar to Linnet, but with less white showing on wings and tail. Longer tail

VOICE: Song similar to Linnet. Harsh *cheueet* call

LOOKALIKES: Linnet (p.239), Redpoll (p.241), Meadow Pipit (p.172), Rock Pipit (p.173)

The Twite breeds in rather barren, bleak habitats including moorland and tundra. In winter it gathers in flocks and moves south to arable land and coastal areas, especially salt-marshes where it often feeds along the tide-line. It eats mainly small seeds. A cup-shaped nest is built among low vegetation. The 4–6 eggs hatch after 12 days and young fly 11 days later. They are cared for by the parents for about 2 weeks. There are 1 or 2 broods.

adult male

adult females

11.5–14.5 cm

| J | F | M | A | M | J |
| J | A | S | O | N | D |

Redpoll
Carduelis flammea

ID FACT FILE

Size: Usually smaller than House Sparrow

All birds: Small black bib, red forehead, grey-brown, strongly streaked, pale underparts, 2 small wing-bars

Northern race: Larger, paler, greyer, pale rump

Male (summer): Red flush to breast

Juvenile: Lacks red forehead

Bill: Stubby

In flight: Light and bouncing. Has circling song-flight with slow wing-beats

Voice: Buzzing trill

Lookalikes: Linnet (p.231), Twite (p.240), Siskin (p.238)

A variable species. A larger race breeds in northern birch and conifer forests and a smaller, tit-like race in the British Isles and the Alps. Northern Redpolls migrate to central Europe in autumn. Redpolls eat seeds, especially birch, and insects. The cup-shaped nest is built in a shrub or a tree. The 4–6 eggs hatch after 10 days and the young fly after 11 days. They are independent approximately a week later. There are 2 broods.

adult male

adult female summer

adult female

juvenile

SPARROWS, BUNTINGS AND FINCHES

16.5 cm

J	F	M	A	M	J
J	A	S	O	N	D

Crossbill
Loxia curvirostra

ID FACT FILE

SIZE: Larger than Greenfinch

ALL BIRDS: Large head, short forked tail

MALE: Varies from orange-red to green, dusky wings and tail

FEMALE: Green-grey, with yellow-green rump

JUVENILE: Like female but heavily streaked

BILL: Large, heavy-looking, crossed at tip

IN FLIGHT: Powerful, bounding. Large head and short forked tail

VOICE: Greenfinch-like twittering song. *Glip-glip* call

LOOKALIKES: Greenfinch (p.236), Scottish Crossbill (p.243)

Crossbills live in conifer woodlands. They move if food is short, sometimes resulting in new woods being colonised. The bill is uniquely adapted for removing seeds from cones. Nesting is linked to the cone crop and egg-laying may take place even in winter. The nest is built high in a conifer. The eggs hatch after 14 days. Young fly after 20 days and are fed by parents for 3–6 weeks.

adult male

adult female summer

juvenile

adult female

16.5 cm

J	F	M	A	M	J
J	A	S	O	N	D

Scottish Crossbill

Loxia scotica

The crossbills that are resident in the remnants of the Caledonian Forest of N Scotland eat seeds from the tough Scots pine cones. They have heavier, stronger bills than the Crossbill and are now classed as a separate species. Their nest is similar to that of the Crossbill. The 3 or 4 eggs hatch after 13 days. Young fly at 21 days and are fed by parents for up to 8 weeks.

ID FACT FILE

SIZE: Larger than Greenfinch

ALL BIRDS: Similar to Crossbill with larger head

MALE: Varies from orange-red to green, dusky wings and tail

FEMALE: Green-grey, with yellow-green rump

JUVENILE: Like female but heavily streaked

BILL: Crossed at the tip. Larger and heavier than Crossbill's

IN FLIGHT. Powerful, bounding. Large head and short forked tail

VOICE: Greenfinch-like twittering song. *Glip-glip* call

LOOKALIKES: Crossbill (p.242)

adult male and female at nest

adult female summer

juvenile

adult female

14.5–16.5 cm

J	F	M	A	M	J
J	A	S	O	N	D

Bullfinch
Pyrrhula pyrrhula

ID FACT FILE

Size: Larger than House Sparrow

Adult: White rump, black tail, black wings with pale wing-bar. Grey back, black cap

Male: Bright pink underparts

Female: Pinkish-grey underparts

Juvenile: Browner, lacks black cap

Bill: Thick, short, black

In flight: White rump. Fluttering in bushes, strong across open ground

Voice: Quiet warbling song. Soft, sad *pew* call

Lookalikes: Chaffinch (p.234)

This attractive species is unpopular with gardeners and fruit-growers because it eats buds and shoots. It also eats fruits and seeds, and young Bullfinches feed on invertebrates. Northern and eastern populations migrate southwest. Bullfinches nest in woods, thickets and hedges. In winter they may visit town gardens. The nest of small twigs is built in shrubs or trees. The 3–6 eggs hatch after 12 days. Young fly after 15 days, and there are 2 or 3 broods.

adult male

adult female

adult female

juvenile

18 cm

| J | F | M | A | M | J |
| J | A | S | O | N | D |

Hawfinch
Coccothraustes coccothraustes

ID FACT FILE

SIZE: Larger than Greenfinch

ALL BIRDS: Thick neck, large head, short, square-ended tail with white tip

ADULT: Pinkish-brown. Black wings with white bars

JUVENILE: Less colourful than adult

BILL: Huge and conical, grey or yellow

IN FLIGHT: Usually high, deeply undulating. Distinctive profile of big head and small tail

VOICE: Weak musical song. Call a loud Robin-like *tick*

LOOKALIKES: Waxwing (p.178)

A very distinctive but secretive finch, which has a huge bill for opening large seeds including kernels of small fruits such as cherries. It also eats buds, shoots and insects, especially caterpillars. It lives in mixed or deciduous woodland and is particularly fond of hornbeams. Sometimes nests in orchards. It builds a well-concealed, bulky nest of twigs rather high in a tree. The 4 or 5 eggs hatch after 11 days and the young fly 12 days later. Northern populations are migratory.

adult

juvenile

adult female

16–17 cm

| J | F | M | A | M | J |
| J | A | S | O | N | D |

Snow Bunting
Plectrophenax nivalis

ID FACT FILE

Size: Larger than House Sparrow

Male (summer): White, black back, large white wing-patches

Male (winter): Much browner

Female and juvenile: Less white than male, with a variable amount of white in wings

Bill: Short, thick, dark in summer, yellowish in winter

In flight: Rather long, pointed wings, white sides to tail, white wing-panels

Voice: Call a musical *teu* or pleasant twittering

Lookalikes: Reed Bunting (p.249)

The most northerly breeding songbird, which nests in the high Arctic or on the tops of high mountains. At home in barren, often icy conditions. Eats mainly seeds. Snow Buntings migrate south to winter on beaches, coastal marshes or open country well away from the sea. They often gather in flocks. The nest is in a cleft in a rock or amongst boulder scree. The 4–6 eggs hatch after 12 days and the young fly 12 days later.

adult male summer

adult male winter

adult female summer

adult female

16.5 cm

| J | F | M | A | M | J |
| J | A | S | O | N | D |

Yellowhammer
Emberiza citrinella

Resident in open countryside with bushes and scattered trees. Characteristically, it sings from the top of a shrub or from overhead wires. Yellowhammers form loose flocks in winter and northern populations migrate south. They feed mainly on seeds, but some invertebrates are eaten in summer. The nest is on or close to the ground among vegetation. The 3–5 eggs hatch after 13 days. The young are cared for by both parents and fly 11 days later. There are 2 broods.

ID FACT FILE

Size: Larger than House Sparrow

Male: Bright yellow head and breast, chestnut rump

Female: More variable, less yellow and more stripy

Juvenile: Even less yellow than female

Bill: Strong, thick, bluish

In flight: Long tail forked at tip. Strong and quite direct

Voice: Call a sharp *zit*. Song a rattling *chitty, chitty, chitty, chee-ezz*

Lookalikes: Yellow Wagtail (p.175), Cirl Bunting (p.248)

adult male summer

adult females

15.5 cm

J	F	M	A	M	J
J	A	S	O	N	D

Cirl Bunting
Emberiza cirlus

A rather shy bunting of small fields and tall hedges, mostly in S or W Europe. Mostly resident, but forms small flocks in winter which often visit stubble fields. Eats seeds, but takes insects when nesting. Sings from the tops of tall bushes. The bulky nest is built low down in a shrub and hidden in dense vegetation. The 3 or 4 eggs hatch after 12 days and young fly after 11 days. There are 2 broods.

ID FACT FILE

SIZE: Smaller than Yellowhammer

ALL BIRDS: Rather hunched when perched. Flattish head

MALE: Yellow and black face, yellow underparts, greenish band on breast

FEMALE: Paler yellow than female Yellowhammer, grey-brown rump

BILL: Stubby, shaded blue-grey

IN FLIGHT: Rather weak with shallow undulations

VOICE: Song a rattle similar to start of Yellowhammer's. Call is a thin *zit*

LOOKALIKES: Yellowhammer (p.247)

adult male spring

adult females

15–16.5 cm

| J | F | M | A | M | J |
| J | A | S | O | N | D |

Reed Bunting
Emberiza schoeniclus

ID FACT FILE

Size: Slightly larger than House Sparrow

Male (summer): Black head, white collar, sparrow-like body, white outer tail feathers

Male (winter): Head-pattern more like female

Female: Lacks black head. Has brown cheeks and pale 'moustache'

Bill: Stubby, blackish

In flight: Direct but a little weak. White outer tail feathers

Voice: Call a soft *seeoo*. Song a repetitive *zinc zinc zinc zonk*

Lookalikes: Yellowhammer (p.247)

The male often sings from a prominent perch in a reed-bed or wet ditch, but Reed Buntings also nest in drier conditions including arable fields. They eat seeds and insects. Northern populations migrate southwest in autumn. The birds form flocks in winter and often join with other small birds on farmland and other open areas. They nest among vegetation on the ground, laying 4 or 5 eggs which hatch after 13 days. Young fly after 10 days, and there are 2 broods.

adult male summer

adult females

SPARROWS, BUNTINGS AND FINCHES

18 cm

J	F	M	A	M	J
J	A	S	O	N	D

Corn Bunting
Miliaria calandra

ID FACT FILE

Size: Larger than Reed Bunting

All birds: Large head, brown streaked back, paler underparts. Streaking often forms patch on breast

Bill: Pale, heavy

In flight: Quite deep undulations. Display involves fluttering with dangling legs

Voice: Hurried, confused jangle

Lookalikes: Skylark (p.166), Yellowhammer (p.247)

A large, rather plain bunting which lives in undulating lowlands, open countryside and on arable farmland. Uses small bushes, large plants or overhead wires as a song-perch. Mostly resident, but forms flocks in winter and sometimes large roosts gather in suitable thickets. Nests on the ground in a tangle of grasses. The 4–6 eggs hatch after 12 days. Young fly at 9 days but may leave the nest sooner. There are 2 or 3 broods.

adult

adult

INDEX

Numbers in brackets indicate cross references in the text.

Auk, Little 143
Avocet (92), 93

Bittern 27
Blackbird (189), 190, (231)
Blackcap (202), 203, (214), (215)
Brambling (234), 235
Bullfinch (182), (234), 244
Bunting, Cirl (247), 248
    Corn 250
    Reed (167), (233), (246), 249
    Snow 246
Buzzard (64), (67), (68), 69, (70), (71), (72), (73), (74)
    Honey (64), 67, (69), (70)
    Rough-legged 70

Capercaillie (82), 83
Chaffinch (182), (202), 234, (235), (244)
Chiffchaff (204), 205, (206)
Chough 226, (227)
Coot (90), 91
Cormorant (9), (10), (11), 25, (26)
Corncrake (88), 89
Crossbill (236), 242, (243)
    Scottish (242), 243
Crow, Carrion (228), 229, (230)
    Hooded 229
Cuckoo 150, (157)
Curlew (113), 114
    Stone 94

Dipper 179
Diver, Black-throated (9), 10, (11), (25)
    Great Northern (9), (10), 11, (25)
    Red-throated 9, (10), (13), (25)
Dotterel (95), 97, (98)
Dove, Collared 145, (146), (147)
    Rock (145), (146), 147, (148)
    Stock (147), 148, (149)
    Turtle (145), 146, (147), (149)
Duck, Tufted (47), (52), 53, (54), (59)
    Long-tailed (47), (55), 56, (59)
    Ruddy (47), 63
Dunlin (101), (102), (103), (105), 106, (120), (122)
Dunnock (180), 181, (182), (209)

Eagle, Golden (65), 66, (69)
    White-tailed 65, (66)
Eider (42), (47), 55, (56), (59), (60)
Egret, Little 28

Fieldfare 191, (194)
Firecrest (207), 208
Flycatcher, Pied 210
    Spotted 209, (210)
Fulmar 17

Gadwall (44), 45, (47), (48)

Gannet 24

Garganey (46), (47), (48), 49

Goldeneye (47), (53), (54), (55), (56), 59, (62)

Godwit, Bar-tailed (111), 112, (113)

    Black-tailed 111, (112), (115)

Goldcrest (180), 207, (208)

Goldfinch (236), 237

Goose, Barnacle 38, (39), (40)

    Bean 34, (35), (36), (37), (41)

    Brent (38), 39, (40)

    Canada (38), 40

    Egyptian 41

    Greylag (34), (35), (36), 37, (41)

    Pink-footed (34), 35, (36), (37), (41)

    White-fronted (34), (35), 36, (37), (41)

Goosander (42), (47), (55), 60, (61), (62)

Goshawk (67), (69), 74, (75)

Grebe, Black-necked (12), (15), 16

    Great Crested 13, (14), (60), (61)

    Little 12, (16)

    Red-necked (13), 14, (15)

    Slavonian (12), (14), 15, (16)

Greenfinch 236, (238), (242)

Greenshank (107), (116), 117

Grouse, Black (80), 82, (83)

    Red 80, (81), (82)

    Willow 80

Guillemot 140, (141), (142), (143)

    Black (140), (141), 142

Gull, Black-headed (24), (126), (127), 128, (136)

    Common (24), 129, (130), (132)

    Great Black-backed (24), (131), 133

    Herring (17), (24), (125), (129), (131), 132

    Lesser Black-backed (24), 131, (132), (133)

    Little (24), 127, (128), (130), (139)

    Mediterranean (24), 126, (128)

Harrier, Hen (71), 72, (73), (74)

    Marsh 71, (72), (73)

    Montagu's (71), (72), 73

Hawfinch 245

Heron, Grey (27), 29

Hobby (76), 78, (79)

Hoopoe 160

Jackdaw (226), 227, (228)

Jay (160), 224

Kestrel (75), 76, (77), (78), (150), (157)

Kingfisher 159

Kite, Red 68

Kittiwake (17), (129), 130

Knot 101, (102), (105), (106)

Lark, Shore 167

    Sky see Skylark

    Wood see Woodlark

Lapwing (92), 100

Linnet 239, (240), (241)

Magpie 225

Mandarin 43, (47)

Mallard (44), (45), 47, (48), (50)

Martin, House (168), (169), 170
   Sand (158), 168, (169), (170)
Merganser, Red-breasted (42),
   (47), (60), 61, (62)
Merlin (76), 77, (78)
Moorhen (88), 90, (91)

Nightingale 183, (185)
Nightjar (150), 157
Nuthatch 219

Oriole, Golden (162), 221
Osprey 64, (70)
Ouzel, Ring 189, (190)
Owl, Barn 152
   Little (155), 156
   Long-eared (153), 154, (155)
   Short-eared (152), (153),
     (154), 155
   Tawny 153, (154), (155), (156)
Oystercatcher 92, (93), (121)

Parakeet, Ring-necked 51
Partridge, Grey (80), (85), (86),
   87, (89)
   Red-legged 86, (87)
Peregrine (78), 79
Petrel, Leach's (22), 23
   Storm 22, (23)
Phalarope, Red-necked 122
Pheasant 84, (87)
Pintail (45), (47), 48, (56)
Pipit, Meadow (166), (171), 172,
   (173), (174), (240)
   Rock (172), 173, (174), (240)
   Tree (165), 171, (172), (209)
   Water (173), 174
Plover, Golden (94), (97), 98,
   (99)
   Grey (98), 99

Little Ringed (95), 96
   Ringed 95, (96), (121)
Pochard (44), (45), (47), (51), 52
   Red-crested (47), 51
Ptarmigan (80), 81
Puffin (140), (141), (143), 144

Quail 85, (86), (87), (89)

Rail, Water 88, (89), (90)
Raven (228), (229), 230
Razorbill (140), 141, (142), (143)
Redpoll (239), (240), 241
Redshank (107), (115), 116,
   (117), (121)
   Spotted (111), 115, (116),
     (117)
Redstart (182), (183), (184), 185
   Black 184, (185)
Redwing (192), 193
Robin (181), 182, (183)
Rook (226), 228, (229)
Ruff 107, (116), (117)

Sanderling (101), 102
Sandpiper, Common (103),
   (106), (118), (119), 120
   Curlew 105
   Green 118, (119), (120)
   Purple (101), 104
   Wood (118), 119, (120)
Scaup (47), 53, (54)
Scoter, Common (47), (53), 57,
   (58)
   Velvet (47), (57), 58
Shag (25), 26
Shearwater, Cory's 18, (19), (21)
   Great (18), 19, (21)
   Manx (18), (19), (20), 21
   Sooty (18), (19), 20, (21)

Shelduck (41), 42, (47), (55), (93)

Shoveler (42), (47), (48), 50

Shrike, Great Grey 223
Red-backed 222

Siskin (236), 238, (241)

Skua, Arctic (24), (123), 124, (125)
Great (24), (123), (124), 125
Pomarine (24), 123, (124), (125)

Skylark (165), 166, (171), (172), (250)

Smew (47), (56), (59), 62

Snipe (108), 109, (110)
Jack 108, (109)

Sparrow, House (181), 232, (233)
Tree (232), 233

Sparrowhawk (74), 75, (76), (77), (150)

Spoonbill 30

Starling 231

Stonechat (186), 187

Stint, Little (102), 103, (106)

Swallow (158), (168), 169, (170)

Swan, Bewick's (31), 32, (33)
Mute 31, (32), (33)
Whooper (31), (32), 33

Swift 158, (169)

Teal (44), 46, (47), (48), (49)

Tern, Arctic (24), (134), (135), (136), 137
Black (24), (127), (136), (137), 139
Common (24), (128), (134), (135), 136, (137), (138), (139)

Little (24), (134), (136), (137), 138
Sandwich (24), 134, (135), (136), (137)
Roseate (24), 135, (136), (137)

Thrush, Mistle (191), (192), 194
Song 192, (193), (194)

Tit, Bearded 211
Blue (213), 217, (218)
Coal (213), (214), (215), 216, (218)
Crested 213, (217)
Great (216), (217), 218, (219)
Long-tailed 212
Marsh (214), 215, (216)
Willow 214, (215), (216)

Treecreeper 220

Turnstone (104), 121

Twite (239), 240, (241)

Wagtail, Blue-headed see Yellow
Grey (175), 176, (177)
Pied 177, (210), (212)
Yellow 175, (176), (247)

Warbler, Cetti's 195, (196), (198)
Dartford 199
Garden (198), 202, (203)
Grasshopper (157), 196
Reed (195), (197), 198, (202)
Sedge (195), (196), 197, (198)
Willow (204), (205), 206, (207)
Wood 204, (205), (206)

Waxwing 178, (245)

Whimbrel (112), 113, (114)

geon 44, (47), (48), (52)

heatear (186), 188

hinchat 186, (187), (188)

hitethroat (197), (199), (200), 201, (203)

Lesser 200, (201)

oodcock (109), 110

oodlark 165, (166), (171)

oodpecker, Great Spotted 163, (164)

Green 162, (221)

Lesser Spotted (163), 164, (219)

Woodpigeon (146), (147), (148), 149

Wren 180, (181)

Wryneck 161

Yellowhammer (175), 247, (248), (249), (250)